THE
FIELD & STREAM
Upland Bird
Hunting
Handbook

The *Field & Stream* Fishing and Hunting Library

HUNTING

The Field & Stream *Bowhunting Handbook* by Bob Robb

The Field & Stream *Deer Hunting Handbook* by Jerome B. Robinson

The Field & Stream *Firearms Safety Handbook* by Doug Painter

The Field & Stream *Shooting Sports Handbook* by Thomas McIntyre

The Field & Stream *Turkey Hunting Handbook* by Philip Bourjaily

The Field & Stream *Upland Bird Hunting Handbook* by Bill Tarrant

FISHING

The Field & Stream *Baits and Rigs Handbook* by C. Boyd Pfeiffer

The Field & Stream *Bass Fishing Handbook* by Mark Sosin and Bill Dance

The Field & Stream *Fish Finding Handbook* by Leonard M. Wright, Jr.

The Field & Stream *Fishing Knots Handbook* by Peter Owen

The Field & Stream *Fly Fishing Handbook* by Leonard M. Wright, Jr.

The Field & Stream *Tackle Care and Repair Handbook* by C. Boyd Pfeiffer

THE
FIELD&STREAM
Upland Bird Hunting Handbook

Bill Tarrant

Illustrated by Rod Walinchus

THE LYONS PRESS

10 9 8 7 6 5 4 3 2 1

Printed in the United States of America

Library of Congress Cataloging-in-Publication Data

Tarrant, Bill.
    The Field & stream upland bird hunting handbook / William Tarrant.
       p.   cm. — (Field & stream fishing and hunting library)
    Includes index.
    ISBN 1-55821-916-1
    1. Upland game bird shooting.   I. Title.   II. Title: Field and stream upland bird hunting handbook.   III. Series.
SK323.T37   1999
799.2'46—dc21   99-10280
                                             CIP

Contents

Preface

And I Do Not Walk Alone

The gun dog world lost one of its best when Bill Tarrant, *Field & Stream*'s Gun Dogs editor since 1974, passed away on November 22, 1998. He was sixty-nine.

Tarrant possessed a rare understanding of the canine mind and often wrote about the complex and curious relationship between man and dog. His total dedication to this animal led him to his most important mission—to end brutality in training—and his relentless assault on those who would beat or otherwise terrorize Pup has changed the face of dog training. Bill was so passionate on the subject that he often said, "People who train with brutality just don't have much fertilizer in their plot."

But Tarrant was no grim reformer. He delighted in the special world of dogs, dog trainers, and hunters, and for nearly a quarter of a century he entertained and informed the readers of *Field & Stream* with a "country-simple" approach that became a hallmark of his writing. It was a deceptively simple style that bore the touch of a master hand.

Bill Tarrant was truly dogdom's poet laureate. If you would like to honor his memory, show kindness to a pup.

> *And you stood there holding this pup close to your cheek, smelling that last-night's ice-cream-carton-smell of him, your fingers sunken into his soft belly, woven through his silken fur, when across your face goes that rough, wet tongue.*
>
> *What you had in your hands was absolute, non-diluted, ever-growing, non-demanding, can't-live-without-you, take-me-wherever-you-go, hurry-back-if-you've-got-to-leave love.* — *"And I Do Not Walk Alone."*
> Field & Stream, *February 1974.*

I edited Bill for eight years, and month after month, he wrote lines I would have killed to have written. But those two extraordinary paragraphs just may have been his finest. Such a simple sentiment, the power of love and how it changes your life. Rest easy, pard.

—*Slaton White*

THE FIELD & STREAM Upland Bird Hunting Handbook

Introduction

WE WERE two skinny kids running behind a hound named Droopy: toe-to-tail to freedom's call. The other guy was K. Bob Greenfeather who lived down the road: said he was Kiowa. We'd side up together, totin' beanie shooters and pockets of pebbles in search of turkeys or pheasants—which didn't exist where we hunted. But the point is, we never hunted little birds, just big birds worth a big brag.

Now it's strange to sit here at evening's half light and recollect that K. Bob died years ago—back East somewhere, an accountant I think. I but close my eyes and see him running once more in that bright Kansas sun.

That's when we caught it, you know? *That contagion that comes with bird hunting.* And now, after fifty years of taking others to field, how many times have I seen it strike again and again. The guest will be an ordinary fellow, belong to a bowling league, play golf on Sunday afternoons, coach his kid through baseball, and help his wife with the heavy spring cleaning. Then WHAM! Right before your eyes, standing in a lespedeza patch or landing on the opposite bank of a creek, the guy picks up the downed bird, holds the warm lump in his hand, and you see the mystical repose settle across his face as he senses the mystery of it for the first time—you know, life and all.

And I know he's succumbed.

Next time I see the bowling ball it's a lawn ornament. The golf clubs have been sold at a garage sale, and his wife took off with the money. He still takes the boy to baseball practice, but going there, and coming back, he tries to convert him to bird hunting.

Which means I must erect a sign right here: BEWARE.

Or you may read this book and go, too.

It Ain't One Bug, It's Many

I rise most days to follow a dog through thicket and bog, up hill and down some hoof-pocked trail, in search of feathered adventure. In one way or another it's always on my mind.

Granted, legal seasons won't let me stay afield like Daniel Boone or Ben Lilly. So a great part of my hunting is in memory: written on paper. Written to help those who may work in factories and skyscrapers: to acquaint them with, and help them enjoy, those few precious hours, or days, they might have afield with a dog.

I guide them through bramble and orchard, show them how to avoid running briar and wait-a-bit bushes, identify fields of rape where a dog can't smell diddly. I introduce them to row crops and spreads of soybeans, patches of sunflowers, sesame fields, and abandoned orchards—all to put a bird in their pocket. I often feel I'm showing them a side of God I know they'll treasure.

For there's some K. Bob Greenfeather harbored inside each of us: out running through a plum thicket, yelling at Droopy to leave that cow pie alone. Man is now 3 million years old in one form or another, and almost every bite he ever took, every quest he ever made, everything that determined whether he lived or died, depended on hunting. And how well he did it.

The Hunt

But the hunt is so much more than sustenance.

It's a limitless kaleidoscope where you're strung tight or laid back, joyful or damned, a hand raised in exultation or a toe kicked in disgust—outwitting the game or being duped and left standing stupid and empty-handed. It's all life in one outing, in one hour. It's birth and death, win or fail, live or die.

It's not a 40l(K) plan. It's not creating a pension, or counting your seniority, or being snug in your tenure. For there are none of those things in a bird field; there are none as a hunter. There are no big boards at the stock exchange where you can list bobwhites.

The hunter's life is a matter of heart and priorities, of living refreshed and fulfilled, of making matters simple and straight and honest.

The author with a snappy English setter and a blue grouse.

It's understanding dog talk more than human ruminations. It's reading rocks and stalks and every quirk of the land. It's knowing where the hummingbird sleeps at night and where it'll first appear for breakfast. It's knowing which way, when startled, the bird will fly and dive and rise.

MOST OF ALL IT'S THE BEAUTY

Hunting: It's the brilliant flash of sumac in a bright overhead sunlight. The quick dart of a small fish in a rivulet as you bend to drink. The jerking back at the sight of a snake laid straight out, dead, on a mound of snow. Or the opossum gone nuts, foaming at the mouth, as it staggers in meaningless circles.

It's driving home from a hunt near Christmas Eve and seeing some candles punch out their cheery light from a farm window. Or spying a feral cat furtively slipping into the brush with a field mouse adangle from her mouth.

It's pulling an apple from someone's tree, rubbing it on your hunting jacket, hearing it crack as you snap off a bite. Walking until you can't lift your feet—having walked so much that season that you've worn out the top of the toe on your boots. And trying to do things right by putting that weather-sealing gunk on them, then putting the boots in the kitchen stove and hearing your wife's garbled dismay.

But it's the surprises. The first snowfall as you lean against a sycamore tree and watch the five-pointed leaves, bright as brass, drift to earth. Or look up suddenly and see a sunset splashed across the unending canvas of the West in crimson, and gold, blue and purple, magenta and orange.

Or kicking the brush to oust a bird the dog has pinned to earth with its intense point, and instead have a doe leap up, glance but a second, and bound away.

Yes, a hunt is so many things that don't involve taking a shot. Like that noon my buddies and I stopped at a convent, entered, and sat an hour listening to the nuns in choir. Not one of us thought of a limit, or felt pressed for time, or fumed that there was no game to be found.

Hunting is a not a mad dash, a barrage of shells, a boasting of power. It is instead thought, study, concentration, fusing with the earth, melting into nature—learning your quarry so well you can predict its location and upon finding it, letting it go.

Your pride is being one with the bird. Knowing the bird as well as it does itself. And knowing your own self. To regard the hunt as a challenge of maturity, knowledge, and appreciation and as a lifetime of love and dedication.

Yes, dedication. It's the hunter who keeps the game in the fields, not the hunting protester. You save and increase what you love. The game has your respect, your care, your ethic of fair chase, and your deep abiding promise not to introduce it to anyone who is a slob.

Never is a bird wasted, or denigrated, or considered less than you because it did not evade the blast of a 12-gauge shotgun.

You would be no more without it than it would be without you. You live for each other, sustain each other.

THEN THERE'S THE DOG

I'd like you to come with me. I've spent many years getting things settled in my mind to visit with you about it. Things other men may not have learned.

And when my company falls short, the dog's won't.

For that is the ultimate magic of bird hunting: the dog. I call dogs God's angels. They do so much for us. They can scent skin cancer, tell a dairy farmer when a cow is coming into estrus, sniff out termites, predict epileptic seizures and earthquakes, hear for the deaf, see for the blind, alert on arson accelerants, bombs, and dope; and take up residence in a care home to lower everyone's blood pressure and lessen prescription intake. The litany goes on and on.

And to think this ultimate gift to us will spend a day with you and me, helping us do something so natural and grand. I can't do any of those fine things dogs do for us. I feel privileged to be afield with a dog.

So if you're ready, let's go. I'm excited to have you along. And the dog always makes good company, even if I don't.

Gimmicks, Gear, and Garb

MY WORLD is God-made-man. I want my life natural—and all that touches it. Man-made-man is the norm today: plastics, polymers, prosthetics, silicon-enhanced and cloned.

Once boats were powered by wind, sleds were pulled by dogs, and big-game hunts were taken on horseback. Now we've got ear-splitting engines and stenchy fuels, and tomorrow will offer some new device that costs 20 times what it's worth and robs us of 90 percent of our outback pleasure.

So I'm going to tell you how to go afield, but you do what you want. Nobody's told me what to do in the boondocks since the Marine Corps, and I accord you the same latitude.

RULES FOR ATTIRE

There are some rules to this game.

1. The ultimate yardstick for hunters is how well they wear their mud. In other words, fancy doesn't cut it: Function does. Wear what works.
2. The most effective and comfortable way to stay afield, bar any fashion designer's notion, is layered. Wear successive layers of light clothing, which can be shed as the day warms or as your activity increases. If you sweat, you're losing it: The test is that simple.
3. Boots are the single most important item you can buy and wear. They must be sure-footed for traction, supportive of your

6

unique feet and ankles, and comfortable for a limitless trek. Young guys don't necessarily need them, but older hunters better slip in orthopedic inserts.

Socks worn with boots must wick away moisture (perspiration), move fluidly with the inner lining, and stay fitted. Forgo the socks that bunch and sag and stretch to two extra sizes.

Thanks to modern technology, boots and socks are now made of miracle fibers and materials. If that's what you want, go for it! I don't. Cotton and wool have sustained us for centuries. Why should I abandon them? As a matter of fact, God chose wool, fur, feather, and leather to cover and protect the birds and beasts—whose world you're entering. Why take less than the best God could give them?

LITTLE THINGS

I once accompanied Hawaiian Watson T. Yoshimoto, Weatherby Award Winner and Bird Dog Field Trial Hall of Fame honoree, on a Mongolian hunt for argali sheep. Yoshi had a master list and a specific location for every item in each of his four safari bags. In the dark of night, he could zip one open, insert a hand, and immediately touch a tube of sunscreen—or sunglasses, lip salve, Kleenex, gun oil, anything he needed.

I always marveled at his packing and his book keeping. And on many trips I had to listen to his repeated logic on why I should become equally accountable. I tried, and over many hunts did improve, but never to match this master of inventory location.

TRAVEL LIGHT

There's seemingly no end to what you can tote. I remember the overweight charge on Yoshi's luggage from Moscow to Ulan Bator, Mongolia, could have paid for his new pickup. But I understood why Yoshi needed all that stuff, since every place he hunted was novel and exotic, and every shot he took was an attempt for a world record. Everything had to be right.

Me? I was looking for adventure and something different to eat for the night's kerosene-lighted dinner.

And I still am. So I advise you to do as I do, and travel light. I'm overloaded with a PayDay candy bar and an apple. If I could take only one thing on a hunt, it would be toilet paper. Second place would go to insect repellent.

THE GUN

I'm not going to be much help for you in this category. I use guns to paddle boats, push down barbed wire so I can get a leg over—I'm only 5 feet, 7 inches—and shuck the shells, then stick out the unloaded gun to steady a buddy who's hung up and tottering in a stream.

Mostly what I care about a gun is, will it shoot? Sure, I'd like the least weight, most balanced swing, and a design that fits perfectly in my shoulder, but other than that, so what?

My favorite gun is not a side-by-side heirloom; no, I want an automatic. I use a lightweight Franchi 20 gauge for bobwhite, for example. And I shoot a Remington 12-gauge auto for pheasants, prairie chickens, grouse, and anything else that takes lead to drop.

I shoot predominantly low-brass 7½s for quail and load a 6, plus two 4s, for pheasants. The theory is that the 7½s will drop the quail from flush to 30 yards, and for the pheasant 6 will have maximum spread for the first shot and long range, with tightly grouped 4s for the go-away hope. Lead has been the hunter's mainstay in shot for decades, but some states won't permit it anymore, even for upland game. Check the regulations.

There's not a type of gun I've not carried afield. In my gun cabinet are over-and-unders, side-by-sides, pumps, even single shots. But as you grow, your needs change. Being there eventually becomes more important than scoring there. And where you once handled complicated hardware, now you want it light and simple. For example, I hate new cameras with too many confusing functions and buttons. And as for rental cars, I can sit in the garage and experiment for an hour before I dare pull out.

I once asked an attendant to help me. He said, "You're in an Avis, I'm Hertz." "So?" I said. He stared at me and explained, "I don't do nothin' with other company's cars." I asked him, "Ever think of just being a good Samaritan?" He thought a minute, and I was on my way. He'd showed me where all the secret buttons were hidden.

Another time in a motel I learned you couldn't turn on the hot tub unless you were sitting in the tub: it took your body weight plus the switch. Oh, for the natural simplicity of a farm pond!

THINGS FOR PUP

And as for the law—I mentioned it before, in regard to the shot in shells—bright orange is now required for bird hunting in most locales. You need it on your cap, shirt, vest, and/or jacket—enterprising retailers even sell it on game bags or shell bags.

You and Pup can share the same water and energizer supplies—that is, if you fill some large gelatin capsules, obtainable from your vet, with honey, and you and Pup pop one about every two hours.

Cactus can immobilize Pup just as though he had a seizure. Carry tweezers to pull out the thorns. Such dogs could use rubber or leather boots, which do work. You tape them to the ankle fur. Other dogs may get tantalized with porcupines; you'll need pliers to pull out the quills.

Wire cutters prove an asset when Pup gets hung up in a barbed wire fence. Oh yes, it happens. And the dog won't take too kindly to you piddling around. Immobilize him with a blanket and cut the wires.

Some dog handlers (especially woodcock and ruffed grouse hunters) want a bell attached to Pup's collar. Others are satisfied with an orange nylon collar. And there's an element who want a beeping collar that you can hear or one that transmits a signal to your electronic receiver. They want to lessen the chances of losing a great dog.

The basic tools for hunting Pup (or training him, for that matter) also include a wide nylon collar with welded D-ring and a check cord ending in a swivel snap. Collar and cord will do it all.

Finally, there's some nonsense being advertised out there. How about a raincoat? Can you believe it? Or how about this: an antenna that attaches to Pup's collar—you can see that thing whipping about way out there. But so can Pup's bracemate, and now you've developed a trailer.

Carry your dog to and from the field in your car. Sure, you can put him in your pickup bed, but I worry about his safety back there. See if you can't get him inside. Knowing the nature of dogs, they'd make sure you were inside if they were the driver.

More will be said about gear and guns and dogs as we go from one bird species to another. Why, heck, we may stop the hunt and train Pup a bit.

Let's get started.

Bobwhite Quail

THE MONARCH of game birds is the bobwhite. This quail has an adulation borne of many things. The familiar call at dawn in the hollow behind the home place. You're taking a break from the hunt, sitting in a country graveyard, eating your lunch, then notice a bobwhite perched on a nearby tombstone. The bird is part of us.

Plus, there's the scat, the burst, the missed heartbeat as the covey scrambles up from a dog's encroachment or a kicked boot. Years ago, during the Depression, you could buy a shotgun shell or two at the crossroads store and hope to drop two "pottiges" after work. That way we could also have quail at dinner.

Those were the bobwhite's tattered subjects, but the titular element secured the bird's crown.

THE GENTRY

There are mansions with manicured savannas all over quail country, great plantation houses bought and dedicated and planted and pathed and fenced and framed by tall pine in continual pastoral murals—just for the bobwhite.

Remember when Hobart Ames, the toolmaker from Braintree, Massachusetts, bought the Ames plantation at Grand Junction, Tennessee, arriving each fall in his private railroad car and entourage to have a go at the quailey bird? The grounds are now the home of the National Bird Dog Championship, run exclusively on bobwhite.

I remember a long-ago noon, walking out on the front porch of the clubhouse at the Dixie Plantation as Mrs. Livingston was delivered by her chauffeur in her black 1937 Chevrolet sedan. She stuck out her wrist for anyone to take and walked with caution into the shack.

She stood a while to catch her breath, to find a propelling strength, then spoke in fractured voice: tinkling and cryptic, like thin, breaking glass, as she wished us all to her Continental Championship. And we all bowed. We were rough men in mud-caked boots with red and white demarcations on our foreheads where our brimmed hats sit day on day as we rode in the saddle, handling bird dogs.

WEALTH

But I'm talking about Mrs. Gerald M. Livingston because of wealth. It seems wealthy people like bobwhite. One handler told me that Mrs. Livingston owned the land under the Empire State Building. I don't know. Maybe she did, maybe not.

The reason I know she was rich was the black 1937 Chevy sedan. I was there in 1975, and no one else had a 40-year-old car. Only the affluent can afford to keep 40-year-old cars on the road, in mint condition.

Well, such vignettes make up part of the bobwhite's royal trappings. Just like John Olin's plantation at Albany, called Nilo. And the physical plant he built and kept to perpetuate this little bird. Plus the wizard he hired for game management: Francis Frazier, an old-time dog trainer. The big trucks loaded with corn, driving the country lanes, the aft propellers splattering corn everywhere for the demure birds to eat. And Francis tending his flash cameras to learn what predators were eating the quail eggs or killing the chicks. Incidentally, it proved to be opossum.

"DAMN THE RICH"

I smile when I hear the poor cuss the rich. They don't know the philanthropy spent on birds or bird dogs, or the knowledge learned by an old scion who wants the best quail hunting in the state. That's where we get our advancements. But many people still cuss them.

I remember when Olin wanted to know what was "killing those damned bird dogs in the kennels." Then he called the veterinary school at Cornell University and told them he was writing them a $1 million check to find out the cause, and how to stop it. That's how the world got the distemper vaccine: all because of bobwhite.

So there's no monarch without subjects. And those are en masse for bobwhite, from the sharecropper to the international banker. They all go afield with a shotgun, a dog, and a hope, looking for that little band of birds at dawn, all bunched up, keeping their heads down, their breathing stopped so the dogs won't smell their breath. (Actually, the dog is scenting the feces the birds have dropped—that's what slams a dog to point in a scent cone, the droppings.)

THE HUNT

To hunt them best, the savvy hunter knows the time of day and matches that to the schedule of the birds. They arise, look for breakfast, dust to rid themselves of minute vermin. If in season, they seek a mate; otherwise they search for cover, especially with an overhead canopy to thwart hawks. Hawks are their main fear. The federal government protects all hawks; is the federal government the bobwhite's worst enemy?

If you find an early-morning covey of quail still circled and holed up from night's rest, just sail your hat over them. Let them but sense the shadow, and see them duck and freeze. Hawks are their doom.

THE DIRT BIRD

Bobwhites are the ultimate dirt bird. They demand bare ground. It facilitates feeding, enhances their ability to see insects, keeps their

Field Trial Hall of Famer Wilson Dunn, from Grand Junction, Tennessee, takes a second bobwhite to hand from a future trial prospect.

feet dry, lets them move about easily, and provides them rapid transit lanes and dusting areas.

Quail spend most of each day walking about, scratching the soil, feeding on the round. Many quail can go days without having to fly. They literally walk from their roost and stay to ground until dusk.

Also, in the spring, chicks will be 1 to 2 inches high. If they were hindered by a heavy mass of grass, they couldn't travel or scratch or peck for food. Chicks must also be kept dry, or they can sicken and die. Bare dirt is the best nursery.

THE EDGE

There are two truths about all game birds. One, they don't dawdle at dawn. It's up and at 'em. And two, they feed at the edge. That is, wherever there's a break in cover, some distinct demarcation between one type of cover or feed and another type. This is where you'll usually find the birds.

They'll be dining in breaks between soybeans and lespedeza. A stand of multiflora roses or a plum thicket will form a hub where quail will feed at the perimeter: wherever one vegetation changes to another, or just to plain dirt, that's where you'll find your covey.

WATER

Quail don't require drinking water. They get moisture from insects, for example, or the dew collected on seeds. But you'll find bobwhites at water sites for two reasons. One, they're there because of the edge that is formed; and, two, because the standing water creates a micro-environment fostering succulent plants, grasses, and insects.

Especially when the land is dry, this means that you must hunt wet. Seek out windmills, water tanks, cattle ponds, irrigation ditches, watersheds, and creeks. The quail you'll find there will not have congregated to get a drink but to eat the vegetation and insect life that survives best in a wet environment.

So now we've learned two things. Hunt wet when the land is dry—and always favor the edge. Keep in mind the best theoretical habitat for a bobwhite covey could be likened to a New Mexican arroyo: dry dust with scattered cover. And believe me, I've found them there. Found them in northeast New Mexico, the Oklahoma panhandle, and all through South Texas.

SPEAKING OF TEXAS

Traditionally, the storied mecca of bobwhite has been Dixie. But the great populations there have now been lessened for several reasons, particularly loss of habitat. Great shooting can still be found, but not like the old days.

Today's bobwhite's burned-up Garden of Eden is South Texas. Bud Daniel, who summers in Monticello, Arkansas, and guides Texas quail hunts in the winter, combines knowledge of dogs, game, and habitat with a continuous patter of colloquial witticisms and sundry hilarity that makes for a mighty enjoyable guide.

Bud looks like a rancher, not a cowboy: He wears clean khakis, not crummed-up denim, has high cheek bones, laughing eyes, a square jaw, a grimed hat, leather gloves, and a check cord stiffer than a lariat. He's good with dogs—knows how to get the most out of them yet still protect them from South Texas hazards—such as slate-dry thirst.

Realizing that waiting out a sentence from Bud is like waiting at the DMV for a license plate, we hear him say, "South Texas bird hunting is a good bit different from classic, textbook, old typical-type bird hunting that people know and remember from days gone by. You know, the old covey rising up the bitch's leg, textbook dog work, all that flawless stuff.

"And if you expect to find that every time on every find down here you're going to be disappointed because that doesn't exist in Texas. Why? Because the weather conditions usually are a lot tougher scent-wise and can change dramatically during a brief period of time during the day."

I recall long bursts from a Gatling gun in a grade B Western each time I wait out a Daniel sentence.

He continues, "It's no gentleman's sport hunting bobwhite down here. It's an aggressive sport. There's no pure dog work. Too much open space, lots of wind, tight places with heavy cover that confuses and confounds the dogs to some extent. Plus birds really move a lot more, which means they're on the run.

"So when a dog points, if he's been broke to death by some classic trainer, he's not going to move, and he won't relocate on these birds when he probably should.

"But if a dog relocates too aggressively, sometime you don't get an early rise because the birds get up farther in front of the dog.

"Then, too," adds Daniel, "there ain't much brush down here and that dog is standing out there naked in the line of fire, for those birds are taking off low because there ain't no cover to protect them. You know, there's just so many things different."

At first I don't realize Daniel's stopped talking. Then jarring myself to attention, and once again eyeing the greasewood flats, I ask, "But why would a bird be here in this desolation in the first place?"

WHY TEXAS?

Daniel answers, "Well, I'll tell you. If you get out a book on poultry and see what the proper way . . . what the ideal conditions are . . . to raise and hatch birds or quail or chickens, South Texas is that. We have vast, vast areas, where one spot may be the size of an automobile and as bare as a pool table; and adjacent to that will be a spot that is so thick you can't cuss a cat in it.

"And that's a perfect situation, for a brooder situation, once a bird has hatched. Also the temperature at the time of the hatching season or the nesting season hovers in the 90s, which is ideal for any quail. Ninety-three degrees would be the ideal. We have a lot of that, plus an extended nesting season. Birds are starting to pair off down here in late February.

"Harvest comes, and they start pickin' cotton in July. The birds have that extended time from February . . . why, we'll see birds that aren't more than two weeks old in late November. And that makes a 10-month nesting season.

"So you've got that extended nesting season. And the ideal conditions for raising birds, both temperature and cover wise. Plus birds don't necessarily want to eat seed. And seed in this country is an alternative to insects and green shoots.

"And until you have a killing frost down here, and we've only had two this winter, you seldom find any seed in a bird. And you never find an extruded craw [now this is important] unless it's been bad, cold weather for a long time.

"Birds don't eat like you and I do. I eat because it's good and I like it and it tastes good and I cram full of it. But birds eat for three reasons: One, for energy; two, for heat; and three, for moisture.

"All this is available in South Texas; plus, birds don't have to move a lot to get it.

THE IMPORTANCE OF KNOWING WHY BIRDS EAT

"Now everything a bird takes in goes to the craw first. But the craws are empty here—which tells us that birds don't need feed for heat. And they need very little for energy, because they don't have to move a lot. So a bobwhite in this country is a full 2 ounces lighter than one in southern Oklahoma and 4 ounces lighter than its cousin in Kansas.

"The Kansas bird has food in its craw because it's eating a lot for body warmth and energy. A killing frost in Kansas takes away the bugs and the shoots, so the quail must eat grain. That's all they have left; they have to switch to seed.

"And that's not ideal in Texas. For a bird will carry its lunch through a partridge pea patch to go to a grasshopper. Bugs and green shoots are preferred."

This back-country wizard with his mile-long sentences has me spellbound. How about you? He should . . . because Bud Daniel knows his business like none other I've ever met.

KANSAS

Now the reason Bud Daniel mentions Kansas is because it's the second premier bobwhite venue in America today. And it betters Texas in view: Those barren flats give way to rolling prairie with running streams, great stands of cottonwood, grain by the ton, and maybe the best ground cover and overstory (canopy) in the world.

I was born there, raised there, and left a toenail under every rock there. Southeast Kansas can produce 20 coveys a day, even 20 coveys a half-a-day.

Plus the cover works easily for a bird dog. There's always a breeze, a mud puddle to flop in, a spring to drink from, a deep bed of mixed prairie grass to lie in and rub away the dust and vermin—and no rattlesnakes to speak of.

You learn things in every country. We always knew we'd hit a covey within 100 yards of a cardinal sighting. We also knew to concentrate on the road's borrow ditches and windmills and abandoned structures. Bobwhites love old houses, barns, churches, and schools.

Most important, Kansas farmers are friendly. If you ask nicely, they'll let you hunt their place. Plus, there are miles of state land open to the public.

But in South Texas, almost every square foot of land is leased. You pay to get on, or you must be invited: There's a lot of corporate leasing.

WHAT ELSE?

What else do we need to know about hunting bobwhites? How about firepower and dog work?

Only moderate power is needed to drop a bobwhite. Shoot a 20-gauge, 28-inch barrel, with 7½ shot and you'll be fine. In fact, 12 gauges might almost be too much for the diminutive birds.

Now for the dog. There are several imperatives in adopting a dog for bobwhite hunting. One, the English pointer, English setter, and Irish setter have premier status; then along comes the Brittany, the less popular setters, and all the continental breeds: the German pointers, wirehaired pointing griffons, pudelpointers, vizslas, weimaraners, and the little known munsterlanders and spinones.

The dog must have intelligence, intensity, endurance, heart, biddability, the desire to please, ample wind, the capability of a great race, and a birdiness that borders on the zany. The hunting dog stud book pick of the lot is the English pointer: It gets the most registrations of serious field trialers. This number has especially picked up since careful breeders have concentrated on congeniality in this breed.

You see, old-time pointers harbored many carnal instincts. They'd be out for birds, jump a sty, kill a pig, then race a half mile to wipe out a chicken coop. But breeders like Bob Wehle, from Midway, Alabama, and Henderson, New York, now produce pups that buyers call back to report, "This dog was congenitally trained."

Yes, trained in the womb? Trained in the gene pool? These dogs are not hardheaded, self-willed. They want to please, and they have the functional conformation to do it.

In a recent issue of *The American Field,* the official field trial newspaper, I counted the name Wehle or Elhew (kennel name) 1,400 times. That's how this remarkable breeding is being rewarded. That's how a new bird dog is being brought to field. And there are others accomplishing similar results. Bully to them.

I wish we could get such ingenious and responsible breeding started in other sporting species.

WHAT YOU NEED

I'm now convinced you shouldn't teach a dog what it doesn't need to know. That's a quote from Montanan Ben Williams, the developer of the prairie Brittany.

You see, Ben hunts 40,000-acre parcels and wants a dog with legs to cover that vast area. So for 30 years he's bred this unique Brittany.

I went to see it. Ben puts them down in packs of four to eight. The dogs train the dogs. The only things Ben requires are that they come when called and honor a point. The reason for this is clear enough: If the dogs are a half mile away and don't honor, there could be a hell of a fight.

Never have I witnessed finer performers.

As a matter of fact, Ben—and other considerations in my travels and my training—helped set my requirements for tomorrow's bird dogs.

They should whoa, point, honor point, relocate, hunt singles, fetch if required by the handler, and self-cast for the next covey. I do not want a mechanical dog. I want a dog that thinks for itself and gives me the benefits of its genetic genius.

I hear people say, "I'm going to take my dog hunting." But it's the dog that takes the hunter hunting. If not, then why don't you go alone?

Today, with all our instruments of brutality, we restrict the dog too much—and we remove too much of the fire. We don't give the dog its head. I don't want such a dog. I want a dog that self-hunts because it knows more about it than I do. Why should I give the orders?

My job is to start the dog right, encourage him to excellence, then get out of his way and let him do it.

What Your Bird Dog Should Do

Just off the bat, he should self-cast for likely objectives. He should know the lay of the land, the best bird-producing coverts, what all that means when put together, then cast to use it.

To train a dog to evidence such savvy and maximum efficiency, you merely work it over endless miles of land and tons of birds. More drills. Just train a dog to hunt by hunting him. And know this: There's no dog problem that can't be solved with a bird.

Some wannabes buy these bird-dog-training videos that never once, I mean it, never once show a bird. Start looking. You'll see it. That's like teaching a boy to become a Cy Young pitcher without touching a baseball.

HOW TO HUNT PUP

In this book we don't train dogs, we hunt birds. There's a way to do it, and this is how.

English pointers and setters are not pack dogs. They're usually hunted alone or with no more than two other dogs down. The traditional setting is one lone bird dog, a hunter, and a long tree-shrouded valley you'd die for.

The dog is at race, searching for scent. When suddenly he hits it and either slams to immediate point or, knowing the scent is faint, moves forward until his nostrils confirm, he's entered his power zone. What's that? That's the proximity where his ability to flat hold the birds slams in, pressing the birds to earth—totally immobilized, so they can't fly. Then the dog waits for the gunner.

When the gunner appears the dog tightens up even more, his body rigid, a bone-and-flesh arrow, pointing to the exact spot where the birds are penned down.

Now this is imperative. We've seen it too often, and it places the dog at great disadvantage. The gunner walks up behind the dog and directly past his side.

The emphasis of the gunner's movement naturally prompts the dog to move forward—the gunner's passing body is too great an incentive. So never, ever walk up beside and past a bird dog. Always go way around, ever keeping your eye on the dog and on the place he indicates the birds are stuck. Then you're ready for the dog to move or the birds to launch.

Such positioning has two values. One, it gives dog and hunter an unobstructed view of the rising covey. And two, it puts the gunner out of the dog's life space so the power of the shot will not produce a gun-shy dog.

WHOA

How many bird hunters know that "whoa" has nothing to do with birds. "Whoa" means for the dog to put all four feet flat and not move an eyelash. "Whoa" is yelled to stop a breakaway, to keep a dog out of a sludge pit, or to rein him in before an interstate.

Never does the hunter say anything around the pointing dog. This is nothing but distraction.

An English pointer flushes a single bobwhite. The bird is directly above the end of the hunter's barrel.

When the gunner fires, the dog can do several things. I want mine to follow the flight and mark the landing of the covey and any dead-fall. Do you know the sport is short on good judges? I know of instances where a mature dog did just this at a field trial and the judge dropped him because the dog was "not steady on wing and shot." The dog knew more about the game than the judge.

The gunner must also mark all birds down in order to help the dog. The hunter tells the dog, "Alright," then, "Find a bird," and the dog searches the cover. Finally, the dog is dispatched to the covey's relocation, or to singles.

When the dog finds a downed bird, he may or may not deliver to hand. The handler will know. If the dog is just going to locate and not fetch, the gunner needs to accompany the dog. The worst thing we can do is drop a bird and abandon it.

When all birds are placed in the game bag, the gunner then calls the dog and inspects his eyes, nostrils, ear tips, and underbelly. If the dog is thirsty, he is watered from a canteen or directed to a creek. Be especially watchful of the dog's eyes. The gunk that can pile into and behind the eye lids is phenomenal. Let that stuff stay there and you may not have a dog that can hunt tomorrow. All you must do is pull out the eye lids and flush the eyes with water. If gunk piles up at the corners, wipe it out with a Kleenex.

THE NEW BIRD DOG IN THE FIELD

For 30 years I've specialized in hunting Labrador retrievers for bobwhite. The results have been fantastic. And the dogs love it.

Ideally, I put down four all-age Labs and cast them for game. Following along, I can control them with a whistle and watch every signal they transmit. When they make game their whole body tells you. The set of the neck, the cock of the ears, the tenseness of the cape of muscle that bows over the shoulder. The tails rigidly tremble, the flanks flex. You know the birds are coming up.

The dogs barge in, more than leap to flesh. Impervious to harsh cover, they'll invade anything, ignore any pain.

But once again, we require here what we required in the bird dogs: great intelligence, birdiness, biddability, and all the rest.

I wouldn't hunt quail any other way, but it may take you some time to get used to such an idea.

THE POINTING LAB

We Americans are crazy about fads and gadgets. At seminars, people ask me, "How can you train with just a rope and collar? The sports catalogs say you've got to have this and that and that."

Well, my belief is that sports catalogs are designed to sell gear, not train gun dogs.

And so it is with the pointing Lab. Sure the Lab points, almost all Labs do, but it is a sight point they give you. And who wants that? To do it, the dog has to so encroach on the bird that he can stand over it and look down and see it. If the bird has any wildness in it, it'll be gone.

God simply didn't put into the Lab what he put into the bird dog. It just doesn't have the remote power that turns birds' hearts to stone, immobilizes their wings, actually stops their breathing. No, a pointing Lab is not what I want. You choose for yourself.

PEN-RAISED BIRDS

Terry Smith, from Decaturville, Tennessee, died about 14 years ago, in a car accident on a winding Tennessee road.

I'll never get over it.

Terry was the consummate outdoorsman and fitted my primary criterion: He wore his mud well. We were hunting one day at Stuttgart, Arkansas, when the mallards caught Terry returning to our blind. He merely sat down in the water.

I yelled at him, "What on earth—you've got mud and water to your chest."

He said back, simply, "I'm duck hunting."

Terry had come by his family's farm and was rebuilding the house, which he discovered was made of solid cherry. The place had survived the Civil War, and Terry and I spent a great deal of time there.

He'd fix something to eat and we'd sit at the gate-legged table and he'd say, "That's brought on." Which meant whatever it was we were eating wasn't raised there.

And that's the way it is with pen-raised birds. They were made by man, not God, and they're brought on.

Yet what gun-dog trainer could cope without them? Pen-raised birds will let you train your dogs, but they'll never have the scat, the wildness, the panic, and the will to survive at all cost as their wild cousins.

One thing you can do to increase their value afield is to make sure their flight pen is planted in the same type of cover as the release area. The birds then make the transition without harboring a need to escape, and why not? Too often, the new cover they're planted in isn't what they were raised in.

The gun-dog pro knows that his charges will encroach too much on the pen-raised birds and will consequently knock wild birds on a real hunt.

Everything has to be adjusted for these tame counterparts.

Many big-time operations build sheds, called Johnny houses, to keep quail overnight and release them each morning. Gradually, the liberated birds take on wild characteristics. And this is good, because it approximates more the conditions found on a real hunt.

Each evening they are called back to the Johnny house by their "call-back" bird.

Other trainers release birds to the wild and leave them there, letting them eat out of specially built garbage cans situated around the training grounds to provide sustenance.

So the pen-raised bird is a mixed blessing. It'll train your dog for you, but not in actual hunting conditions. You take your best shot with these birds and go with it.

CLOSING HOUR

Sundown comes to every hunting day. Time to quit. And that's where we are with the bobwhite. No bird on earth is as much fun, as exciting, as fulfilling to hunt as this bird. He is the monarch.

I hope we've given you a leg up on your next outing. Remember, bobwhites are found on the edges, around water. They are the ultimate dirt birds, so look for clear areas where they can feel safe and comfortable. You won't find them buried in a tall sedge field.

And before you ever go to seek them out, remember to steel yourself. They come up like rockets and scatter like fragmented hand grenades. That's their defense, designed to scoff at your gun and leave you standing with wilted pride and gaping mouth.

Pheasant

IF A PHEASANT would suddenly turn human, you'd see him riding a Harley-Davidson, wearing a Wehrmacht helmet and sporting an open, black leather vest with assorted silver chains hanging here and there. Across his forehead would be tattooed the words, *"Make My Day."*

The pheasant is a belligerent and pugnacious bird that lives its whole life on the edge of mortal combat. When in cramped captivity, the pheasant's beak must be cut off or shrouded and his leg spurs kept short, for he can stab like a marlin and kick like a mule.

He keeps about six wives, either to his joy or his headache, and lives in a military caste system. And know this: The cock is no bird to be admired by any women's group. When pressed by a gunner, he pushes the hens to fly to save his own skin.

Mike Gould, gun-dog trainer extraordinaire, has kept flight pens with 10,000 of these birds on hand for game preserves he's managed.

He tells the story about how he once had a prime pheasant cock-bird left over after training and decided to reintroduce it to the flight pen. The bird was dead within seconds after entering the pen, killed by his brethren for assuming he could place himself anywhere in the hierarchy he liked. The bird had attempted to retake his old rank, and died because of it.

You don't mess with a pheasant. Remember that the next time you send a Lab pup to fetch one up. The pup can be ruined for life if the bird decides to make a fight of it.

What to Do with This Scrappy Bird

We hunt him, that's what. Here's how.

The ring-necked pheasant is a big bird, some 36 inches in length, though 22 to 23 inches can be in his tail. He weighs about 4 pounds and he's mostly meat. He can be found across the United States, though South Dakota has made a fall business of them, with birds and hunters by the thousands. The important pheasant bird-dog trials are usually run somewhere like the Finger Lakes region of Upstate New York.

The birds were introduced to this country in Corvallis, Oregon, in 1886. The American counsul general in Shanghai, Judge Owen Denny, secured the birds and successfully shipped 20 to 30 of them to his brother's farm. Several years later, a wealthy sporting family in Alamuchy, New Jersey, hired a Scottish gamekeeper who brought a few of the birds with him. So now they were started on both coasts, and today they range from Maine across to Oregon, poking south some places as far as New Mexico, and generally following the terminus of the repeated ice glaciers.

I met and fell in love with them in western Kansas. You don't find them in eastern Kansas, and game biologists tell me it has something to do with lack of lime in the soil.

What an Opening Morning

What's really special about pheasants in Kansas is the morning of opening day. You can place a toothpick in the ground in Kansas, drive

Mike Gould, a gun-dog trainer from Kamiah, Idaho, lowers his gun to drop a pheasant. Note the intensity of the English pointer.

away, stop 10 miles distant, get out and look back—straight at it. Which means you can see forever in western Kansas. And there are good people to look at out there.

What I'm leading up to is the church or school or community breakfast. Even on the blackest of nights, you'll see glowing lights in the distance. The nearer you get, the greater and brighter they become. You're driving smack dab into the greatest bird-hunting treat in America: The morning pheasant breakfast.

You stop the car and there will be hundreds of hunters milling about in the dark, some exercising their dogs, others taking a smoke, some yelling at others, all happy, all dressed in bulky hunting clothes. Dust is everywhere, in great slow swirls as car after car passes by. Then a door opens and a great flood of light pierces the dark and silhouettes the surroundings.

You enter. There before you, in jaunty aprons and peached cheeks, are the farm wives, the church women of west Kansas, serving breakfast. You're directed here or there. A donation plate poses at the start of the feed line. You look down a groaning board of grub.

You want 16 pancakes? Take them. You don't want scrambled eggs, you prefer poached? "Well, just a minute and I'll have them cooked for you." There's French toast, fruit in season, slabs of bacon, ham, and plump sausages, plus coffee, tea, milk, and juice. It's the west Kansas pheasant breakfast and the greatest event I've attended in my far-flung hunting life.

The money raised goes for choir gowns or school books or maybe a park bench by the courthouse. It's all good, mighty good. And you walk out of that little white, wooden church, or school, or whatever, and you know, it really doesn't matter if you get a bird that day or not. To me, that's hunting.

THE BIRD IN FLIGHT

The cockbird in hand looks nothing like he does in flight. The hens are dirt colored for concealment, but up close the cock pheasant is as dazzling as a jewelry display in Bangkok. What you notice most is the ruby patch at the eyes, the copper breast, the yellow beak, and the iridescent glory of his head. At a distance you mostly see the white ring about his neck.

Jim Culbertson, my dog-training and hunting buddy in Wichita, Kansas, plus Robby Rupp, a teenager who helped me with the kennels, and I were pheasant hunting on a private road near the Quivira National Wildlife Refuge by St. John, Kansas.

Jim was always ornery. A high-school football coach, he delighted in rousting young bucks. So what we'd do is wait until Robby went to sleep in the back seat; then Jim, who was uncanny in spotting a pheasant's white neck ring in the weeds, would slam the brakes on, bang his hand on the outer door, and yell, "Robby. . . a pheasant in the ditch . . . get him."

And Robby, a 6-foot-tall string bean, all angles, would try to untangle himself, get his gun, and fall out the door. Then Jim and I would laugh, slap our knees with our fists, and tell Robby, "There ain't no pheasant," and laugh and laugh.

We did it often because Jim had such great credibility in finding pheasants and Robby had total faith in him. But one time, when once again there was no pheasant, Jim went into his act, Robby went falling out of that door, and bam, a cock pheasant as big as a bomber and as colorful as Mardi Gras erupted in flight—beating its wings and twittering its long tail—right by my open window. I gulped as I watched Robby bag the best pheasant of the day.

Robby stood by the car's front bumper and displayed that big bird and would not get into the car. Jim started the engine and told Robby if he didn't quit showing off he was going to run over him. Those really were good days.

Hunting is not about killing. Hunting is camaraderie, getting acquainted with other hunters, working new dogs, viewing the country in all seasons, picking up pebbles or unusual pieces of bark to take home. And all the tomfoolery . . . that's hunting.

How to Hunt

There are two recognized and established ways to hunt pheasants. Form a row of mates and walk a field in line, pushing the birds before you. When the birds run into blockers at the end of the field, they're forced to take flight.

The other way to go is just you and Pup, and maybe another person with a dog, hunting prime habitat.

The driven hunt is an adaptation of the European method of drivers pushing the pheasants toward a tall stand of trees and having the sports, usually standing on the mowed grass lawns of some grand estate, waiting on the far side of the trees for the high, passing shots. A gun bearer stands beside, ready to thrust a loaded gun into the sport's hands, and to take the one that's just been emptied.

The drivers are usually village boys waving long-poled flags, interspersed with Labrador retrievers, who kick out any sleepers.

There is little sport to the whole mess.

The American drive is more democratic, and fairer to the birds. Yes, the hunters drive the birds, the birds run to the edge of the field and then fly. The drivers walk in a sag, with point guns at each forward edge to get the birds flying out the side of the field. Some pheasants begin loitering before the drivers and at first chance double back. This is where the dogs are supposed to fill the gap.

Now all this can be a pretty hairy undertaking because when the drivers meet the backers and both are armed, there's a lot of shooting going on. Safe shooting is at a premium: Always know where your muzzle is pointing, and never shoot until you're sure that no one is behind your target.

I gave up driven hunts a long time ago, but you should know they are the social event of the west Kansas season. Farmers or villagers will invite all their relatives and friends from several states to join them, rent all the local motel rooms, and have a two-day party. They are a lot of fun.

In the old days, so many birds were taken to hand that the local women would set up shop in their garages and clean birds for so much apiece. Everyone enjoyed the bash, most town people made money, and those invited had great fun.

You and Your Dog

I appreciate the solitude and the quiet wonder of nature by trekking along with a dog, or two or three. We know what we're doing. We stop and kick about every hay mound, stack of cut limbs, or piled-up mounds of weeds.

We especially walk the shorelines of duck marshes, where pheasants idle in the tall salt grass out of the wind, but are near the varied harvest afforded by a water environment.

Pheasants have a passion for borrow ditches filled with weeds. Usually there's ample cover, and run-off underfoot. If you come across a barbed wire fence loaded with tumble weeds, this is prime pheasant habitat. So are Osage orange hedgerows. This is impenetrable cover, and pheasants can lounge in there, knowing full well that the leavings of a row crop field are but a few steps away. Row crops: You'll find pheasants filling their craws there all times of day.

DOG WORK

The state-of-the-art pheasant hunt comes after a big snowfall, when there are great mounds of banked snow. The dog moves before you— he knows his business—as he searches for blow holes. Such holes are breathing tunnels for pheasants that have dug beneath the snow and idle there, with the snow being their insulation.

When the dog detects a blow hole he immediately leaps and bores in, nose pointed to penetrate and scoop. The startled bird will burst free with a cackle, frantically cupping the wind with its wings. It's to no avail. The dog will catch the bird mid-air and you'll laugh and suddenly feel warm all over, for you've just seen bird hunting at its best.

THE DOG

Traditionally, all retriever breeds have been called on to find and control pheasants. The Lab performs excellently, although the golden has the reputation of being the top upland game-bird retriever. The Chessie is a bulldozer and can produce birds where others can't due to his boldness and thrust. And that's not to forget the flat coat retriever. This mellow people-pleasing bird hunter will fill your freezer and vie for a spot in your bed.

Only the retrievers are usually worked on drives, but all of the retrievers plus the spaniels and bird dogs can be used for the one-person, one-dog hunt.

A classic pheasant hunt is turned in by the English springer spaniel. How many photos have I taken of this vest-pocket contender, springing several feet off the ground, with the frenzied pheasant striving to rise above the dog snapping at its tail.

At trial the English springer spaniel is tested on pheasants and ducks, so those two birds are regarded as his primary interest and capability.

Realize there's always an extra bonus from any gun dog: They're

An overloaded Brittany delivers a pheasant rooster to the hunter.

not with you just to kick out and fetch birds. The English springer spaniel is the jolliest bird dog on earth. He is in perpetual laughter and keeps you the same way. Lucky is the one with a sure'nuf hunting springer.

English pointers, English setters, and Brittanies are also tested at trial on pheasants. They are recognized masters with their skill and effort. Plus, all the versatile gun dogs from Europe are prized for their capability in handling this bird.

THE GUN

The pheasant gun is any 12 gauge, with 28- or 30-inch barrel(s), modified or open choked, shooting No. 6s and 4s. Birds are usually shot within 40 yards, but at English springer spaniel trials I've seen Chuck Dryke, and others, drop birds with low brass as far away as 80 yards.

I once told Chuck that his gunning was amazing, and he replied, "You ought to see my boy."

I went to Sequim, Washington, just for that purpose. The boy, Matt, shot the skeet range from the hip, riding a unicycle. He dropped all birds.

So it came as little surprise Matt became America's first Olympic gold medal winner in skeet.

But I'll never forget *Field & Stream* challenging the copy I submitted, saying Chuck could drop pheasants at 80 yards. Though I took an oath before them, the story came out, ". . . 40 yards."

ENOUGH SAID

This rough-out bird, the pheasant, is the common man's sport and meal, though I've hunted him, and dined on him, in banquet halls where French kings once dined.

The pheasant lives just outside the city limits of many towns, and any kid can get to him on a bicycle or by foot. He's easy to hunt, if you've got legs, and though it may take 10 miles to bag one, it's worth it.

The pheasant also does well when raised by hand. When released, he shows more wildness than other pen-raised birds. He is beautiful in hand, fascinating in the wild, and delicious on the table. Seek him out any chance you get.

Chukar

Y OU'VE GOT TO LOVE PAIN as much as birds to hunt chukars (pronounced chuckers), the desert dwellers. Why is that? The bird lives in remote barrens, usually on 90-degree slopes, in regions where temperatures often hit 100° F; he's not prone to set to a point; and when he's not running, he's diving downward with the wind.

The wild chukar has minimal resemblance to his tame cousin hunted on preserves. Yet the chukar is one of three game birds in the United States that can be successfully raised in captivity and released to the wild or used to stock commercial hunting operations.

Wild chukars are rim-rock birds, looking down from their lofty perches, probably laughing at most people's futile efforts to climb up

and get 'em. But that can be their undoing in the most delightful bird hunting of all.

You need to train a hunting retriever on hand and whistle signals, cast him up the canyon sides, get him on a ridge where he will start hunting just as a flusher or a bird dog, then whistle him back toward the rim where any chukars nooning up there will be forced to leap off and sail straight down to your waiting gun.

That's right, chukars take off angling upward, but when airborne, dive in a glide to the valley floor.

All this gets even more exciting if you and your friends and your retrievers float-hunt one of the great western rivers such as the Snake. You drift along, checking the rims, and when you feel there's a chance for success (or you hear their *chuck, chuck*), you launch your dog, cast him up the incline, and wait for him to push the birds to you.

The fun part is floating along in that raft, butt and legs flat to rubber—same way you wait in a lay-out boat for ducks—and seeing the birds come zooming down. Hopefully you'll be on smooth water with no rapids when they get within range, and you'll be able to take your harvest.

Of course, you have no bird until the retriever climbs back to the canyon floor, then you direct him to the fall. And that may be on the bank or wherever the bird's floated up ahead of you, or possibly hung up on vegetation and moored where you were when you shot.

The Lab is not the only dog to help bring chukars to hand. All the retrievers, sundry bird dogs, spaniels, and the many versatile hunting dogs can get the job done. It's interesting to note that field trials are run on chukars in Idaho and other western states. The dog of choice there seems to be the German wirehaired pointer. Some hunters believe this dog's rough coat serves as armor against desert hostility.

When you do get this bird in hand, you'll find little discernible differences between sexes. Both males and females weigh about 1½ pounds and are some 12 inches long, with black chestnut rally strips down their sides, a hooked beak, a white head with a black slash that runs through the eye and curves down and around to the chest, and a gray-blue body, with red legs.

There was a time when the desert had few game birds. Then Ira Kent, of Fallon, Nevada, read an article in 1934 about hunting chukars in the Himalayas in India. As he read a description of that country, it reminded him of his own state. So he got in touch with a friend in the import-export business and inquired about getting some chukars shipped from India.

It wasn't long until his intermediary located 100 chukars for $600 in Calcutta. Now let's put that in perspective. My dad was an electric motor winder in 1934 and, drawing journeyman wages, he was making $14 for a 60-hour week. Dad would have had to work 43 weeks to buy those birds! That's a ton.

Those 600 chukar were stowed on a tramp steamer and shipped to San Francisco. Only 13 of them arrived alive, but those 13 were the basis for the majority of chukars you now find in Utah, Wyoming, British Columbia, southern Alberta, Baja, Idaho, western Colorado, Montana, eastern Washington, Oregon, New Mexico, northwestern Arizona, and western South Dakota.

I'm not saying Kent is the sole party who one way or the other seeded all those birds. Other chukars arrived at later dates from other parts of the Mideast. But Kent was the pioneer. He showed it could be done.

Nor did Kent just go out into the desert and let 13 chukars fly to the wind. No, he set up a "poultry" operation and began raising chukars. These were then *sold* to fish and game departments, which released them at selected points.

It's the same old and glorious story of the hunter funding the fish and game departments' costs for stocking game in American wildlife habitats. It's not the hunting protester, not the anti-hunter who denies the natural order of the wild food chain, or others who've not thought things through—it's the hunter, as always.

In Nevada alone, more than 13,600 birds were released in 30 years. In 1941, a hunting season was opened. Chukars require free-standing water, so Nevada then stopped planting birds and invested in guzzlers. The one-thousandth guzzler was completed in early 1996 (they are placed about a mile apart).

Some states didn't enjoy Nevada's success in introducing chukars. Arizona, for example, has tried hard to establish huntable populations, but presently all plantings have been marginal except in the Arizona strip north of the Grand Canyon.

I've listened to many an account of a hunter shooting a departing and downward-diving chukar on the north rim of the Grand Canyon, then walking to the edge and seeing a gray puff snagged on a naked pinion limb 100 yards below. Over the side the hunter goes. I'm

A hunter stops to thank his Lab for good work on this chukar.

telling you, that's dedication. Ever look down the perpendicular side of the Grand Canyon?

One way to get your bird without hanging by an arm from a rock ledge is to hunt the flats. Well not the flats, exactly, but the rims where the edge drops straight down to the canyon floor. And always look for cheat grass. It bursts forth bright and lime green in the spring, grows a foot tall, and then dies. That's how this grass gets its name: It tricks us with a spring promise and ends up cheating on us with a stand of dead thatch. But chukars love it. If you hunt the cheat grass, you'll eventually bump into the desert dweller.

Chukars also favor sagebrush, horsebrush, rabbitbrush, and spring perennials such as Russian thistle, red-stem fillaree, and fiddleneck. Know your arid grasses and desert scrubs, and you can focus your hunts on specific habitats and cut down on your walking. And make no mistake, the chukar is the ultimate walking bird. I've been on hunts that went 10 miles, with much of that being up and down. And what was brought to bag? Maybe two birds.

But again, don't lose hope. Chukars have a trait you can use. A flock may evaporate upon your presence, but a couple of birds will often remain behind to reassemble the covey. Look hard, get your dog in for a close hunt, stay intense. You may find the remaining birds and get the only flushing shot of your life on chukars.

Too many shots are far behind the departing birds. Chukars are just that spooky, and they have the defense of the ledge. Up, out, and down they go with your string of shot biting clear air and eventually dropping to the canyon floor.

The last tactic to use in bringing this bird to table is hunting the water sources. Subpopulations take up residence adjacent to water-holes and leave track coming and going. Follow them, and you might intercept their makers.

It stands to reason with the heat, the habitat, and the inclines, you want to travel light. Wear layered clothing, carry a lightweight gun, pack some salt tablets and energy bars, and keep your dog and yourself well watered.

About that gun. Few hunters double on chukars. And the few who have tripled should be in some kind of hall of fame. Given a choice, I'd recommend carrying a light automatic. Load the number of shells you want, but considering the weight carried in high heat and the fact that I've seldom seen more than one chukar downed on a covey rise, I often insert but one shell.

Side-by-sides or over-and-unders might give you a make-up shot, but, again, why carry the weight of an extra barrel? Twelve-gauge shotguns with 30-inch barrels are preferred for the long-range punch of a fast-disappearing bird.

Boots have got to be the best for chukar hunting. You're walking on volcanic ash, disintegrated granite, pulverized sandstone—in a way, you're sandblasting your footwear. And you're climbing, so the soles should have good lugs—something that won't slip. Your ankles will be strained and contorted, too, so the tops have to be supportive.

Then, too, you need sunscreen, a wide-brimmed hat, sunglasses for all the glare, and a wet bandana around your neck.

Finally, you'd better know where you are and where you're going. Topographical maps can be life saving. You look at the desert and say, "Why, I can see all the way to Yuma. I won't get lost." Ha! Just go up and down a couple of canyons, top out, and tell me where you are. You can get lost fast in the desert.

You'll have fun pursuing chukars if you use good tactics. The birds are beautiful in hand, and they're worth the try. And they have few equals on the table. Enjoy!

Gambel's Quail

W E'VE LEARNED that bobwhite live in close proximity to humans; Gambel's quail do the same. I lived eight years in the Sonoran desert, where they nested each night in my dense backyard pine. Later, I moved to the piñon-and-juniper high desert beneath the Mogollon Rim at Sedona, Arizona, where each evening the birds roosted in the many pinion that surrounded my place.

The roosting ritual requires a landing area where the birds can scan the trees, then glide to a limb and rustle about. They repeatedly give a four-point *gonk* call as if they're never certain that every-

one's checked in. But all through the night you can hear one or more of them emit soft location calls, telling I-don't-know-who, "I'm over here."

I was always cautious in going about the place after dark because those quail would spook to my movements; not seeing well in the dark, they could have hurt themselves flying about.

Gambel's quail are family dedicated, with the rare distinction of having the male tend the hatch. I've actually seen Gambel's males try to lure a hatch away from a hen or abduct the peeps in her absence. If the female dies and leaves a motherless clutch, the male will incubate the eggs.

They are also beautiful birds, with the cock sporting a jaunty black plume that tilts forward and bobs when he walks. The male is gray, with black and white rally stripes down his sides, a fawn back, and a belly distinguished by a black patch. The hen is dirt colored, but she does sport the plume and racing stripes.

Both birds weigh some 6½ ounces and miss being a foot long by 1 inch. Their flight speed reaches 40 miles an hour, and they can hoof it out at 15 mph, but prefer a moderate-paced walk. It's a delight to see the hen leading her brood through short cover, the peeps scurrying along in disarray like erratic little golf balls.

THE HUNT

Experienced hunters agree it would be impossible to shoot out Gambel's quail; that is, render it extinct by overhunting. The primary reason for this is we hunt a phantom bird. You just can't find Gambel's quail if they decide to avoid you. Consequently, there's usually a generous limit allotted each hunter.

If you do chance upon them and fire on the covey, you will seldom get a second chance. You're primarily shooting young birds, and this baptism under fire creates a life-long spookiness.

Why are they so hard to find? The reason is that they will usually run first, then fly over limitless expanses of heavy cover and stumbling blocks—such as lava rocks and arroyos—thus presenting the hunter with incredible challenges. The birds can thrive on the flats, but prefer hilly country that eventually defeats those in pursuit.

VITAMIN A

Game-biology research in Arizona has determined that the amount of vitamin A in a bird's liver determines the following year's hatch. And the quantity of vitamin A depends on the amount of rain falling from October through March. The rains sprout the green seeds, so the birds can eat well early on. Incidentally, Gambel's are 90 percent vegetarian.

This early feeding triggers their reproductive system, so they pair off and hatch. If there's no rain, there's scant reproduction.

Favored spring foods include the flowers and leaves of Indian wheat and exotic filaree, with a lesser interest in the leaves and flowers of mesquite, paloverde, and mimosa with such legumes as locoweed, deer vetch, and lupine. The preference for these winter annuals continues through the summer rains.

In fall, these winter perennials dwindle—which, in turn, triggers a great dispersion of the quail families. This results in an intermingling of coveys, which manifests itself to the hunters as a "horde" of birds on a covey rise.

Gambel's quail can be found during hunting season on warm hillsides where early rains have prompted fresh growth of green annuals. The birds will also frequent salt blocks at this time because of an increased diet of mesquite beans.

A QUEER TRAIT

Gambel's quail are extremely territorial. Kick up a covey in a particular ravine and you may kick up four more in the same spot during season.

The birds have a queer trait when selecting a safe-haven site. If you find, loft, and fire at a covey, the birds will fly to a preselected safe haven. But—and this is the key to their doom—should you sit and wait for their assembly call, then go and kick up the relocated covey at this new site, the birds will freeze in immobility and panic.

Why? Because you've found their one and only chosen hideout, and they have no place else picked out to go.

Consequently, whereas you usually see Gambel's quail take off afoot, now they flounder in great confusion, with some birds flying far and others landing close. You can tell that each of the birds is very concerned and frustrated. This is when you can achieve the maximum harvest, if that's your interest.

FIREPOWER AND PERSONAL COMFORT

Depending on the mood of these birds, one day you'll need a 12-gauge, 30-inch barrel, open-bore shotgun shooting No. 6s, while other times the birds will stick tight and linger so you can take them with a 20-gauge, 28-inch barrel, modified choke, shooting No. 7½s.

Imperative to any Gambel's quail hunt is the best boots you can buy. The terrain is quite uneven, often hard as coleche, with great scatterings of lava rocks, steep arroyos, and punitive cover. Ankle support proves as necessary as foot tread.

Clothing should always be layered, and that's especially true on any desert quail hunt. You'll leave the pickup in a sort of cold nip, but by 9 A.M. you'll already have removed clothing, even down to a T-shirt.

Primary equipment includes water bottles or canteens. An old army cartridge belt with several canvas-covered aluminum canteens will prove vital for both you and Pup.

Call your dog(s) in often, and water him by pulling a bottom lip out to one side and pouring water into the pouch so the dog can lap and ingest all the water instead of spilling it about.

Finally, don't forget tweezers for removing cactus from Pup's pads. Yes, I guarantee you it'll be there.

DOGS

I've seen almost every breed of dog on a Gambel's quail hunt except a flusher. The dog favored by hunters who actually live in the desert is the German wirehaired pointer. These people believe the dog's rough coat turns the cactus and sundry harsh brush. Another bonus with this dog, they say, is that you can take it atop the 2,000-foot, sheer drop-off, Mogollon rim and hunt it on ducks. Thus, you can have an upland game hunt and waterfowl outing all in the same day.

Web Parton, a gun-dog trainer from Oracle, Arizona, removes spines from a setter on a Gambel's quail hunt.

ADDED BONUS

Hunting Gambel's quail beneath the Mogollon Rim in Arizona can be a beautiful and inspiring experience. The distant spires and turrets and towers of the red rocks, set against the ocher and rouge colors of the never-ending cliff, played out under a spectacular sky continually altered by the radical winds that collide with and bounce off the cliffs, gives you a background that truly could not be bested in any paradise.

There's no hunting in the Grand Canyon, but this is the nearest thing to it, which should give you some idea of the awesome splendor.

CHAPTER

Mearns Quail

REMEMBER Ben Rumson, the prickly misanthrope in the musical *Paint Your Wagon?* Ben sang a song with a stanza that went, "The only hell I know is the hell in hello." Mearns quail sing the same refrain in their sky-high Garden of Eden—as far from humans as these quail can get. I love 'em.

Exotic and imperiled, Mearns have adopted a high-altitude habitat that is one of America's finest hunting venues.

The birds' traditional grounds are the northern, high Sonoran desert of Mexico, with a small spillover in Arizona and, less frequently, New Mexico and Texas. You'll find the greatest concentration of these birds east by northeast of Nogales and south by southeast of Tucson.

Mearns generally live 4,800 to 5,100 feet up, in lush-grass, park-like country, among scattered live oaks and pines, with colossal stands of manzanita that are remarkably hearty, as evidenced by trunks as thick as a man's wrist.

LIFE DATA

An understory of grass is vital for this bird's survival, which seems remarkable when we remember the bobwhite as a dirt bird. We'll get into the Mearns' ground-cover preferences in a moment.

It's practically impossible to push the Mearns from its beloved woods. And without 10 inches of rain each summer, there would not be sufficient moisture to sustain the grasses and forbes that make up the birds' necessary food and cover.

Because thick, heavy grass is their preferred habitat, the birds display the remarkable behavior of squatting amid cover for concealment. That works, but if caught on flat, bare dirt, they'll do the same thing—which is totally dysfunctional.

They have, of course, acquired advanced grass-crafting skills, to the extent the hen will nest her clutch beneath thick grass; when departing, she'll flip over a thatched grass door for concealment of the access hole.

RESPONSE TO POINT

When forced to leap from their squat position, the birds, though strong runners, will go only a short distance before squatting again. When flying, they can attain 20 miles an hour in a short time, but will not sustain the flight, typically lifting over the nearest rise, then touching down in cover.

The experience of my dogs, and myself, is to continually push the birds before us, always guessing which way they'll turn when they top a hill.

Mearns emanate a soft congregation call throughout the year, but the call has a misdirection quality, and one can zero in on it only by walking and "talking" with the quail, especially the females.

DESTRUCTION OF HABITAT

Overgrazing of livestock in the Mearns' range, plus devastating summer droughts, are the enemy of this magnificent little bird. I have personally walked through lands so trodden by cattle that the cover is shorter than nap on a pool table.

Considering these quail are especially fond of nut grass—where they must actually dig the nut from the earth to consume it—the disappearance of cover foretells the disappearance of the species. With our present range policy, this bird will one day be extinct in Arizona and other hard-put locales, and the only way we will be able to see a Mearns, or hunt a Mearns, is to enter Mexico.

THE BIRD THAT CAN'T CLUTCH A LIMB

I have mentioned the unique way this bird dines—it digs. To do that demands long, strong nails. A consequence of this foot structure is that the Mearns cannot curl its claws about a limb and nest aloft. Therefore, it is grounded evermore in the tall stands of grass.

If cattle stamp out the vegetation or rip it open to drought so it easily dies, what does the poor bird eat, and where does it sleep? For it to survive, cattle simply must be removed from this bird's range. Doing this will not be easy.

To vouchsafe my findings, no less an authority than Aldo Leopold, who extensively worked the Mearns' range, concluded in a 1957 resource paper that "grazing destroyed the birds' food resources." It possibly was outside the scope of Leopold's interest at that time, since he said nothing about it, but Mearns also refuse to nest on overgrazed land, further diminishing their potential population.

THE DOG

Mearns are too well hidden and squat too tight to be chanced upon by a lone foot hunter. A pointing dog is required.

A close-working dog that works near the gun—either due to genetic disposition or training—will be the greatest producer. Since the birds are so deeply buried and so capable of turning to stone, it takes a meticulous performer to ferret them out. The dog must painstakingly hunt every inch.

That's not to say a Mearns' hunt can't be a fast-paced adventure. I've had a covey rise and depart over hill and, while pursuing it, have kicked up other coveys on the way.

But really, who wants this? Taking one or two of these birds is sufficient. After all, we're talking about a premier game bird, one that is severely imperiled.

Even to get that one bird, you have to avoid treeless areas. The birds just won't be there. Hunt uphill in the morning—that's the direction in which the birds feed—and cover the canyons come evening. Mearns avoid crests.

When kicking out a covey, expect the same startling explosion you get from bobwhites: Mearns do depart, and depart fast. Watch where you drop any birds, because in this heavy cover your dog may need help in finding the fall. It's rare to be able to watch a covey down, as there are just too many promontories for the birds to loft over and disappear.

Understandably, this is not a bird handled well by flushers or other breeds taught to flush. A pointing dog is the ticket. The same gun and ammo used for bobwhites is used here. The same goes for sturdy boots, layered clothing, and toted water for you and Pup.

THE BEAUTY OF IT ALL

This is one hunt that must be recorded with film. Take along a light-weight camera. The country is that gorgeous. It's also heavy with sandburs, so carry your tweezers for Pup's comfort.

One way to maximize your walk through Mearns country is to look for sign: scratched or dug earth with gashes some 2 inches long, 1 inch wide, and maybe 3 inches deep. Some lucky bird found a nut there. These diggings will be all over the place. Look for fresh ones, which will indicate that birds may be nearby.

In ending our hunt, I'll share this with you. This bird is proba-bly the most magnificently marked bird in our country. He has a dramatic white and black series of swirls about his sparkling black eye, which have earned him the name "harlequin" or clown. Clown, because of all the gaudy make-up such performers use. Atop the Mearns head is a russet shock of feathers, most unkempt in appearance, which, along with those swirls, also encompasses his eye.

The back of the bird is striped black and brown, and the breast is salt and pepper. Altogether, the appearance is just dynamic.

The bird weighs 8 ounces and extends 8 inches, but he has a puffed-up appearance, shaped more like a ball than a bird.

The crown jewel in hand: the Mearns quail.

Visit this bird at least once, just to see him. Admire the country he lives in. Shoot him if you must, but make it the shot of a lifetime.

A Couple of Things I Want to Visit with You About

Back in 1900, 90 percent of all Americans lived on farms. As near as I can calculate from the most recent census date, 4 percent are still there today.

The difference this has made in our lives is dramatic. The boy going to bring in the cows 100 years ago heard the covey of quail, saw the cock pheasant flush and sail over the farm pond. While driving cattle in New Mexico, he saw the scaled quail scatter before the herd; while riding fenceline in the Kansas flint hills, he witnessed the great flights of prairie chickens over the gate. The locomotive engineer going cross-country from the Dakotas to Montana delighted in seeing the Hungarian partridge pace his speed.

In other words, we lived with nature, we were neighbors to wildlife. Today we're often far removed.

When you live with wildlife, you learn to respect it, to know its nature, and you get a kick out of seeing if you can outwit it—and that's hunting. To know a bird or animal so well that you can predict what it's going to do, to be there waiting for it when it's finished out its play—that's hunting.

Hunting is not how well you shoot but how smart you think, and how much you revere what you're after. When you reach this plateau, you really respect the game, and you make sure it's always given an even chance.

What I'm leading up to is that the farm boy of the past was hunting birds as soon as Dad cut the stock off a single-barrel shotgun. He toted that gun to school, either carrying it in his arms or tied to a horse's saddle ring, and during recess he hunted just outside the schoolyard. He also hunted all the way home come afternoon.

No one questioned the right to hunt: It was born with you, like your umbilical cord. Nor was any thought given to taking a gun to school, for how else were you going to harvest the bird?

Yes, it was different, and in many respects a simpler and far better world. Everyone lived by subsistence in those days. The chickens in the barnyard were killed, the hogs in the sty, the steer in the pasture, and the wild birds down by the creek.

So think of the advantage the farm youth had then, the mind set that was given him at birth. This made us a different people, living with a different set of facts. Compare that with the hunter of today. What boy at 10 years of age has harvested everything within 10 miles of his place, or participated in the group festivities that sometimes accompanied hunts: the early church service, the picnic before the hunt, the barn dance that evening.

I was part that boy and part of what we raise today. I could duplicate my uncle's best in the field, have Mom tell me just how many birds she needed for company dinner, and fill her order. I lived for the hunt.

You can still do that today. There are enough weekends, enough game, enough vacations accumulated: You've just got to make plans to be in the field.

Don't think we've lost anything, because we haven't. It's still out there, and you should be, too. You can even work in an occasional game preserve for a change of pace and alternate hunts between upland game and waterfowl as populations of these birds wax and wane.

If I hadn't hunted as a kid, I really don't know what I would have done, what I would have been. Hunting's been the primary determinant of my life. It's taught me to accept challenge and defeat, to have the good sense never to underestimate the other party, to always act within the rules of the sport, and to realize the best of me is when I outwit my quarry.

These are good guidelines for living, I think. Anyway, I don't feel those guidelines have ever failed me.

So hunt. Be a better person because of it. And never forget to invite the new kid moving in down the block to participate in the magnificent world of outdoor sport, at your side.

Another Thing

This high country where you hunt Mearns quail is one of the best of all worlds. Take the time to see it, to participate in its many variances. The Western bygone villages of Sonoita, Mexico, and Patagonia, Arizona—such lyrical names—are the hub of a Mearns hunt.

I've not been there for a while, but there are several startling discoveries at Patagonia. There's the Feedlot Restaurant, where once hung a sign that read, "If you can't control your children, leave them outside." The Last Gasp saloon is just across the railroad tracks to the south, and built around that structure is the Stage Stop Inn. The dining room in the inn has never failed me or any guest I took there.

To the west of all this and a little north is Patagonia's bird sanctuary. I've sat there many times in the summer and listened to the faint melodies. North of Patagonia, on Highway 83, is the world-famous Madera canyon, one of America's greatest bird havens.

That Day with History

South of Patagonia on the dirt road to Lochiel is the first recorded site of a black and a white man crossing the Mexican border into Arizona: 100 years before Plymouth Rock.

Estaban, a Moorish slave described as "Black, massive, and spectacular," who adorned himself with fur trappings and strings of tinkling beads, walked between two giant dogs (some say they were coursing hounds), and for a while convinced the Indians that he had magical powers. But was eventually stoned to death by the Zuni for favoring too many of their young women.

Estaban guided Fray Marcos de Niza, the revered Franciscan missionary, into what would one day be *Norte Americana.* I never hunt Mearns without stopping near the cross at Lochiel, where Estaban and Marcos are assumed to have crossed into present Arizona, and pray for the day, the past, tomorrow, and all that's lovely.

If it fills your needs, double back to Sonoita where there's nightlife in a cowboy blow-out bar, with stamp dancing, line dancing, and noise enough to split the building in two.

Heading back to Tucson, stop at the Santa Rita abbey where the nuns celebrate noon mass in choir. I've sat there, entranced and stunned at their beautiful voices, long after the nuns had left.

All this is to say that good hunters are multidimensioned people: Tough but gentle, hard on themselves but not on others, at peace with the world and wanting to share the best of it, fitting best where there is silence and long shadows and the gentle hints of something far more than wind in the rustling leaves.

You'll not go wrong being a hunter. The legacy assures you of that. For without having been hunters for 3 million years, humans would not have survived and civilization would never have existed.

Scaled Quail

THERE . . . SEE THAT! Yeah, way up there . . . maybe sixty yards? Looks like clods of dirt rolling along. Well, Pardner, you just spooked your first covey of scalies.

"What? Are they always that far away?"

"Yes . . . or farther. You don't get a point on scalies unless you've overtithed at church and refuse to take the refund."

"What?"

"Is it always this hot?"

"Yeah . . . or hotter."

"You want to know why we hunt this bird? Because of the sport . . ."

So it goes with one of the strangest bird hunts on earth—going after the faraway bird, the marathon bird, the "I don't want anything to do with man" bird.

THE BIRD IN HAND

When you get a scalie in hand—and that may be once or twice in a day's hunt—you'll find they're larger than Gambel's quail: some 11 inches in length and 7 ounces in weight. Master runners, scaled quail have thighs like pit bulls.

The back and wings are gray (some hunters say blue-gray, which may be a regional thing), with an off-white breast and a head crest. Incidentally, that white head crest is the source of their nickname: cotton top. Their other name—scalie—comes from the feathers on the breast, which look remarkably like the scales on carp.

PREFERENCES IN COVER

Scaled quail prefer scant vegetation, and you'll rarely find them in thickets as you would a Gambel's quail. The scalies preference is limitless greasewood flats: miles of monotonous, flat ground, with a few cuts or arroyos the birds don't want to cross—so they run with the depression.

The only other time you might be on scalies' land is in answer to some far-removed developer's ad for "40-ACRE RANCHETTES," with assured installation of utilities, but date unknown.

HOW TO HUNT

To hunt this bird you need maxi-power in dog, gun, and legs. You've got to have a dog with a stretched-out quest, one that doesn't mind quartering an eighth of a mile on a cast and can keep up with birds that'll run even farther.

The dog must be an intense English pointer for my money, with the ability to slam to a point with the same intensity a border collie puts a rank bull in a pen—otherwise he'll never plant these birds.

A Llewellyn setter spots a scaled quail hiding on the other side of a "Mickey Mouse" cactus.

A point has to have that quality to it, that power. It has to make a bird freeze because it senses the power of the dog, no matter how far that bird may be from its hiding place. I've seen it often with border collies: the EYE!

With border collies, first the sheep turns but slightly away. There is at first nervousness, then there is a show of futility, and finally the absolute crumbling to the collie's will. The same should happen with birds, especially scalies. The dog must bury them with a glare.

That's not going to happen on the first point. No, when the birds are discovered, they scatter like the start of a Grand Prix. The dog relocates, actually chasing them like an unbroke pup.

All during this race the covey—which can be up to 100 birds—is losing individuals to each side. But the race goes on until, finally, the birds stop and freeze. Even now the pointer usually can't hold the birds. They bust again. Only after the ensuing race will they eventually give up and freeze before the dog, having no more run in them.

This is when you get your shots. You'll seldom drop more than one or two birds, though, as even now they'll flush far out in front. There is the prospect of hunting down singles, however, and now the dog must change from a long-range pursuer to a steady, close-working pointer.

I've hunted scalies from horseback. I've hunted them on foot. I've chased them with pickups. You gain no advantage, no matter how you go. During my heyday, when I could outwalk a Jeep, I finally gave up and hunted scalies only in conjunction with Gambel's. Simply, the scaled quail is a bird that will humiliate you.

WHY HUNT SUCH AN ELUSIVE BIRD?

If the bird is so tough, why is it hunted at all? One reason might be that there are hunters everywhere, but not enough game. There are places in New Mexico, for example, where if you don't hunt scalies, you don't hunt. So the hunter puts on his boots, grabs his gun, releases his dog, and spends a day in the desert with whatever hope he can muster.

DISTRIBUTION

Scaled quail are located in southeast Arizona, northeast Arizona, and central-eastern Mexico (the Chihuahuan desert) all the way to the east-west mountain belt. The birds also inhabit Texas (west Texas and the panhandle), southeast Colorado, and the Oklahoma panhandle.

FAVORITE VENUE

Scalies' favorite venue is semidesert grassland and adjacent lands where scrub has invaded but not taken over. In fact, whenever the cover gets too heavy, too massive, too tangled, these birds hit the road. They eschew promontories and broken-up country and stick to open plains, mesas, and low, rolling hills.

The birds will use scant vegetation for cover, even nesting under a cholla cactus. You'll also encounter them close to abandoned dwellings, feed crops next to semidesert grassland, and irrigation

You'll probably never see another photo of a scaled quail in a tree. The author's hunting companion flushed this bird to a tree; the author was directly underneath.

sites. Scalies will drink water if available, but it's not necessary to sustain their existence.

The birds' favorite elevation is 3,500 to 4,600 feet, with some extreme differentiations, such as the highlands of northeastern Arizona.

REFINING THE HUNT

So far I've given you a gross picture of chasing these running birds. But they also mess around and give the hunter an advantage or two. For one thing, the alert hunter can hear their calls. And even though most quail calls have a ventriloquist disorientation, casting your dog to such sites won't get you a point, but it will get the birds running.

During hunting season, most calling is done to gather members of the covey. There are also alarm calls, which are fairly impossible to describe in print. Just stay afield long enough, listen carefully, and you'll soon discriminate what the different sounds mean.

UP AND AT 'EM

You can also try to follow the birds' daily routine. They arise each morning and start foraging along ridges toward water. But they sleep in different spots each night, so you won't find them today where they were yesterday, and they don't go to water every day. After the morning routine, the next thing on their agenda is to scatter across a slight slope and dine. Midday they seek shade, where they dust and loaf until it's time to snack before turning in.

Most scalies prefer to congregate around stands of catclaw, mesquite, mimosa, and prickly air, so pay special attention to such areas.

Scaled quail also issue what I suppose you'd define as a content call. They'll be foraging along and you'll hear a buzz among some of them—like people in an old-world plaza on market day. You can stand your ground, and they may even start to surround you. They won't stay for long, however.

After stringing out a covey, and lofting it several times, then hunting singles, you should sit—even up to an hour—and wait for the reassembly call. While grouping, these birds will fly far beyond your gun's knock-down capability if aroused, so wait, and wait, and wait. Then cast your dog.

By this account you know you need a high-power pointer, along with a high-power gun to hunt scaled quail. Carry a 12-gauge whatever, with an improved cylinder, shooting No. 7½s.

By now your scalie hunt should be finished for the day, so drop elevation, get into the tough and tangled stuff, and seek out some Gambel's quail.

I've had more than a few two-bird scalie hunts. Don't expect much more than a long walk. But it isn't all that bad. In fact, sometimes it's a lot of fun! Good companions and good dogs make any hunt a joy.

To me, getting one scalie can be as hard to do as doubling on woodcock. When you get one, you can be proud, because you will have earned it.

CHAPTER **8**

Mountain Quail

Y OU AND I just hunted some quail that we couldn't catch up
to, and I suppose there was a sense of frustration, or futility, in
doing that. So the question is, would you go again? Would you
hunt a quail you can't find?

It's the mountain quail, the phantom bird, one that lives in vertical country, where the cover is the toughest, most tangled, thickest
mess of all. It's a bird that'll spook on a California mountainside if it
senses your pickup leaving Nevada, and it will attempt every sub-
terfuge to avoid detection before it will fly.

We didn't know what we were doing, Cosbone and I. We were two young Marines, putting in our time on the base wrestling team at the El Toro air station near Santa Ana, California.

I was reading the football scores in a newspaper and saw an article about hunting California birds. One bird it highlighted was the mountain quail, a bird it said could be invisible right before your eyes.

That sounded exciting to me, so I talked Cosbone into borrowing a shotgun from a sergeant who lived off-base, bought some shells and licenses, then headed north by northeast to get this ghost quail.

We had no dog (they were not allowed in the barracks), but thought nothing of it. We figured there wasn't anything we couldn't handle. And it made no difference that we had only one gun: we'd just hand it back and forth.

I'd read about a forest of giant trees, and when I told my mother about them, she said I ought to go see them so I could describe them to her.

It was a beautiful drive, up through the Sequoia trees, with the great slanting shadows, and through the breaks you could see a hazy kind of blue horizon, stretching forever. We read a sign by the road that said one of those Sequoias was growing before Christ was born.

I told Cosbone that the hunting article said mountain quail migrated from 10,000 feet in summer to the valley floors of chaparral in winter. We figured we were too high for the birds in this big timber at this time of year, but we'd be losing elevation when we doubled back toward Modesto and started around the north end of Yosemite.

We drove the remainder of that day, and the next morning were northwest of the park and heading south. The article said mountain quail could be found from Yosemite Park to the eastern slopes of the Sierra.

We started asking field hands if they'd seen any mountain quail. Most didn't know what we were talking about. Some pointed farther east, and others pointed back west.

We finally stopped at a one-pump filling station that sold bait, beef jerky, soda pop, fuzzy orange work gloves, fan belts, and a little bit of everything. This station owner knew exactly what we were talking about, and sent us down the valley, where he told us to turn right and we'd find the birds everywhere.

He told us to pay special attention to standing water, for these birds drank a lot, and also to look for the meanest bushes we could imagine, for these birds had tunnels in there and could run like hell through them. He also said the birds were spooky.

You know how you just sense things? We didn't stop where the farm improvements were worth anything; instead, I picked out a sort of galvanized gray clapboard shack with an old car in the yard, drove in, and asked if anyone was home. A guy showed up and looked us over. I told him what we wanted and he said, "Sure . . . just go out back there and poke around. Go far enough and that's all public land. You may find something."

We told him we were much obliged—as I said, we didn't know what we were doing—and started mountain quail hunting. What I want you to know is if we had known what we were doing, we'd never have thanked anyone for pointing us to mountain quail.

We walked and climbed and sweated and sat and then, when we heard some bird calls in what we later learned was manzanita—catch it on fire and it'll blow up like a can of gasoline—we tried to bust through it. It wouldn't budge, so we got down on all fours and peeked through the cracks, and sure enough, there were some birds movin'. When Cosbone yelled, "Get 'em," they all vanished.

We sat and looked at each other. There was no way this hunt could be done. Finally, we decided that if the birds were in this manzanita, we'd split up and come in from both sides. That'd bottle 'em up. Ha.

We couldn't find them to start with, and when we did we had to crawl on our bellies through their tunnels. When we came out the other side, or met in the middle, the birds were gone.

I was from Kansas and Cosbone was from Nebraska, and we were accustomed to birds that played the game right, birds that'd jump up right before you and yell, "Get me if you can." Those birds would give you a chance. They weren't this sneaky nonsporting kind.

The plan was to camp out and eat mountain quail, but we never saw one. We substituted red beans and caught a few fish that we cooked and ate with lemons squeezed over them.

We were just kids being kids. We went off half-cocked and ill-prepared. The point is that we went. We now had one leg up on hunting a very elusive bird. If someone stopped us now and asked about hunting mountain quail, we could sure tell them more than we could have a week back.

That's the way it is with all hunting. Each outing teaches something important, reinforces what you've learned before, and gradually you start to get it right. And you never forget the good times getting there—even crawling around in manzanita tunnels and running head-on into Cosbone.

We were back at El Toro watering the football field come Tuesday morning. Then that afternoon it was back to wrestling practice, with never a mention of mountain quail.

WHAT WE SHOULD HAVE KNOWN

Process servers and bounty hunters may have perfected the techniques to bring the wily mountain quail to hand. The average bird hunter never has.

It's best to hunt the more obtainable valley or California quail (same bird, two names), which occupies the same area during hunting season, and pick up the odd mountain quail.

NO DOG

Don't think a dog will do you any good. Dogs can't get through those tangles either. A retriever would be the only dog that could help you, and that would be to fetch any deadfall you might have lucked out on.

To put all this into sharper perspective, you should know the mountain quail is the largest of all North American quail. Measuring some 11 inches in length, the same length as a blue-wing teal, they weigh in at 8 ounces, which is two more than the bobwhite.

DESCRIPTION

A magnificent bird, I feel it out-glamours all others. The male has a chestnut throat and flanks with black and white markings, a gun-metal head and neck, a chestnut forehead framed by tawny side stripes, an olive back and—this is important—a long, straight, drum major head plume.

This plume is twice the height of a plume on any other quail and is composed of two straight feathers, appearing as one, that stick straight up. Compare this with the topnot quail, which have a teardrop plume composed of several feathers all compacted to resemble a great teardrop that bobs over the forehead.

The hen is similar to the cock, but more dusty in overall appearance.

HABITAT

Favored habitat of these birds during hunting season is dry mountain flanks, brushy wooded areas, chaparral, and manzanita. You'll find them among juniper, willow, wild rose, cottonwood, mountain sage, bush grass, antelope sage, and rabbit brush. They'll roost in a piñon tree or any shrub that's over 5 feet tall.

Mountain debris such as fallen timber, charred remains from a fire, and logging leavings get their nod during the summer months at high altitudes.

HABITS

These quail prefer vegetable food, opting first for seeds, fruits, greens, buds, and sometimes roots. The males have a loud, distinct, clear call and will sometimes answer a hunter's whistled inquiry. The male also shares the male Gambel's penchant of doting on the young and even sitting on the nest.

HOW TO HUNT

Experienced hunters physically climb, drive, or ride horseback to get above the canyon walls that quail often prefer. It's a process of walking the ridges, listening for volunteer calls, looking in bare spots, and then whistling in hope that a male will answer.

A dog can only help you by bringing deadfalls to hand. Therefore, the favored hunting dog is the retriever.

Once you hear the quail's call, you drop to all fours and start inching down the drop-off—going slow to minimize falling rock and gravel, going slow to maintain watch for any signs of birds relocating within the dense brush.

Don't think the birds won't know you're coming: They will.

Ken Osborn, a flat-coat retriever specialist from Sacramento, California, takes a break before continuing his hunt for mountain quail, which scramble vertically.

They'll be tensed for escape, so be ready. Chances are they'll run, but pray for that scant surprise of a covey flush (usually some 12 birds).

The one constant in all this is not the size of the covey, or the denseness of the cover, but the verticality of the descent. It'll be tough, straight up and down.

Response of the Bird

Since this is a fast-trigger bird, the covey will usually kick up at some 40 yards. A full-choked 12 gauge with long-carrying No. 4s or 6s is in order. But if the terrain is just too much for you—and it is for me— carry a lightweight two-tubed gun instead. Try a No. 7½ in the first barrel and a No. 6 or 4 in the second.

Should you get a bird, I'd advise you to forgo the barbecue and get it to a taxidermist.

Distribution

California is not the only home for these birds. They can also be found in northern Baja, eastern Washington, Idaho, Nevada, and Oregon. They always choose the best weather, like snowbirds who can afford to winter at Yuma. They'll migrate upward in spring and return to the valley floor in winter. This makes them one of four migrating upland gamebirds: They have the same vertical route as blue grouse, while mourning and white-wing doves cover the country when they move.

A Final Warning

With all that crawling about you're prepared to do, let me leave this last thought with you. The mountain quail's favorite California habit is also the place of choice for the diamondback rattlesnake. You'll find him in the manzanita, too. Have fun.

California Quail

THIS QUAIL seems to love people—or at least what people have done to the land. You'll find him in your backyard, gardens, farmers' crops, city parks, and anywhere there is water. What's more, you can find plenty of these birds. During hunting season it's not unusual to bump into California (or valley) quail in flocks of 500. Wouldn't that blow your mind to see that many birds rise?

Apart from suburban life, you'll find California quail thriving in coastal brush to inland chaparral. To maximize your contacts, hunt for them in creak bottoms, irrigation ditches and tailing ponds, tangled brush, open woodlands, chaparral, grassy slopes, windblown stacks of dry vegetation, canyon rims, grain fields, and vineyards.

DESCRIPTION

California quail have a black plume atop a bold head pattern outlined in white, with a gray breast, striped russet sides, and a scaled belly. The hen, as always, has less distinct patterns.

This quail weighs some 7 ounces and measures 10 inches in length. It cruises at 40 miles an hour when relocating, but if shot at will hit speeds up to 60 miles an hour.

BEHAVIOR

The bird is a strong runner but will flush to a dog and a gun. As with Gambel's and mountain quail, the male helps with the young, and should the female disappear, he will incubate the eggs.

HABITS

Only 3 percent of the bird's diet is vegetable, while the rest of his intake is made up of seeds and greens. The bird has a distinct call that seems to say *Chi-ca-go,* and seems mighty proud telling you about it.

RANGE

California quail inhabit lands from Baja through Washington and inland to Idaho and Nevada. They nest on grass, roost on limbs, rise early to eat and drink, and then, like bobwhites, seek over-story to dust, loaf, and sleep out of harm's way.

HUNTER RATED

Hunters favor these birds over others because of their sportiness. They shock you with explosive rises, quick take-offs mixed with all types of tactics, including putting some upright obstacle between the two of you. The birds will land only to run and fly again. You're not going to come by them without a well-thought-out, concentrated effort.

FAVORED BIRD DOGS

A pointing dog works California quail picture perfect. He often sees them, hears them, and smells them all at the same time. Everything is going for him, which will prove nerve-wracking for a pup. But a seasoned dog will revel in it. And what about those massive, thunderous

This Brittany pup can't believe how many valley quail are running directly in front of her.

coveys of 500 birds? That dog will be telling his grandchildren about this hunt for a long time.

TRAINING

All the dog must do to help bring this bird to hand is honor the scent cone. The moment he detects birds, he must stop, put all four feet flat to surface, and not move an eyelash. Should he doubt the incoming communications and edge forward, crowd the birds, or even take a step, it's likely he'll bump the covey before the gunner is ready. California quail dogs must be rock-bottom steady. Any pointer or setter gives you the best assurance.

I've seen Brittanies, most of the German pointers, plus the standard English pointers and setters afield for California quail. As always—I mentioned this up front—desert hunters favor the German short-haired pointers because their dense, wiry coat acts as armor in a land that stabs, sticks, and pricks.

RETRIEVERS

I've often said the trained retriever can be cast out and around the covey, then worked back to push birds straight to your gun. Much of that is the experimental stuff that I enjoy doing, and a guy out for dinner is better off just putting a meat dog on point and getting his shots.

GUNS AND AMMO

Distant covey rises are common with this bird. Carry a gun bored for modified choke, shooting No. 7½s, or switch to full bore and No. 6s if the birds are coming up too far in front.

When hunting desert birds, it helps if you love steep hills, sheer cliffs, dusty creek bottoms, high chaparral, brush piles, and any other kind of mess that saps your energy, desiccates your body, and belabors your knees until you can't lift them two inches.

Of course, you could always buy a home in their range and hunt in your backyard. Settle in your hammock with a cool one, and keep looking. Your dog can be sleeping beneath you, so both of you can move fast on any sightings—or that clear call of the California male telling you, "Hey Sport, you've got to be kidding."

Prairie Chicken

P RAIRIE CHICKENS are birds of constant winds, inhabiting the great, mixed-grass prairies of mid-America. This is land with few outcroppings of rim rock, or even table rock, where the wind has scraped the dirt clean or the buffalo herds rubbed it naked long ago.

The only trees found on the plains are cottonwood, sandbar willows, maybe some salt cedar, and an occasional sycamore—and then only in the creek bottoms, safe from drought, and free from fire that the wind hurls across gaps in the land.

The country is not noted for rain, but when it comes it's mad about it, pounding the land with hail and heavy water, with the wind trying to knock down all the fenceposts. Snows hit this area hard,

too, and it takes some time to melt because of the deep cold and the insulation of the grasses.

Only cattle are found on these prairies. Nothing else ever came there or happened there. On the edge of oddities is the realization that Remington, the great New York cowboy and military artist, tried homesteading at Leon, Kansas, running a herd of sheep.

The good people of the community convinced him to return home after several roof-lifting parties that cut against their stern ideas of propriety. Remington's property was close to a place called Cow Creek ranch, where I lived for a time with my gun dogs.

I never tired of it there. There were bass in the pond, good grass for the cattle and horses, vast vistas, and no one calling but the mailman. I caught a cattle rustler there and felt for a minute like I'd earned kinship with Earp and Dillon.

But back to the birds.

CHARACTERISTICS

Prairie chickens are big birds, and there are two distinct members of this species. There's the greater prairie chicken, found sketchily from Canada to the Gulf Coast, with the greatest population being in Kansas; and the lesser prairie chicken, which is more concentrated in Oklahoma and down through Texas.

The "greater" of the two is 18 inches long, and the "lesser" is 2 inches shorter. They respectfully weigh 2 pounds, 3 ounces, and 1 pound, 12 ounces (all figuring done on males).

A yearly ritual sees the males gather on booming grounds for courtship rituals, with the hens looking on. The males stamp their feet, puff up their neck feathers, posture, fight, drum the air with expanding air sacs on each side of their necks, and fan out their tails. It was all this that gave the American Indian his macho pose and his powwow. What Indian dancer doesn't have the bustle harking back to the chickens' expanded tail feathers? And how about the Indians' circle of drums, forming a booming ground?

The greater cocks are mottled brown and gray, with black-rimmed stubby tails that expand for showmanship and ritual. They have several feathers on their heads that become upright and rigid when posturing, and on each side of the neck is a booming sac that is bright orange when displayed, but otherwise concealed by long tufts of feathers.

The lesser cocks are lighter in color with red air sacs.

Both subspecies rely heavily on grasshoppers, supplemented with leaves, fruits, and insects, for their survival. Winter sees them switch to seeds and waste grain.

How to Hunt

It's a rare event to get a point on chickens. You can try. I have. But early in life I switched from bird dogs to Labs that just ran through the country and bumped them up. It wasn't that gross. You can read a Lab and know exactly what he's thinking, what he's planning, and what's confronting him. It's all there: the angle of the neck, the perk of the ears, the trembling tail, the tense stance, up on the toes, looking down for sign. Plus it'll glance back impatiently, checking to see exactly where you are, actually managing a look of disgust, dancing and maybe whining a bit to hurry you up. All this means the birds are about to break. You see, the dog and you are bonded, joined at the hip, ESP. The dog itches, you scratch. You're one soul, one mind, one heart.

Ideally, you sight the chickens from far away, cast the Lab to them, then whistle the dog back into the birds. But that's the ideal: Usually the birds break out to the side and re-enact *Gone with the Wind.*

Prairie chickens post sentries, compounding their security by nooning on top of knolls with unlimited views of their surroundings. Canada geese do the same thing on winter wheat. Again, you can try concealment: Drop down and crawl through the grass, then come up the steep side—if there is one—and have the strongest wind imaginable at your back, to cover your noise.

But there's another way, a better way. You can ambush them on their way to breakfast.

The Wonder of Soybeans

You spend a great part of summer getting up before dawn and driving the country roads in chicken country. Finally, you begin to spot the great early morning flights. The birds must leave their roosting grounds—the great knolls—and cross farm-to-market roads to get to grain.

Pick the flight you feel you'll have the greatest success with, and that'll be the flight heading for a soybean field. Along that road there'll probably be a fence row, and mixed into the barbed wire will be lots of tumbleweeds or other vegetable debris.

The opening morning of chicken season, you, your dog, your buddy and his dog wait in the wan light for the first flights. As they come, you check legal shooting time, getting ready, rubbing your palms.

Now they rise and come straight at you, maybe 30 yards straight up, angling to the wind. And *wham, wham, wham* the guns bark, and the momentum of the shot birds carries their dead weight on past you—maybe 200 feet behind you—and you cast the dogs for the retrieves.

FIREPOWER

To get this bird, shoot a 12 gauge with heavy-duty No. 4s or 6s. Your barrel should be 30 or 32 inches, bored full choke. My friend, Jim Culbertson, the Wichita, Kansas, high school football coach, is an amazing long-distance shot, and I have seen him repeatedly bring prairie chickens down at 80 yards. Maybe you can, too, though shots under 40 yards should be the norm for most shooters.

It's been my experience that prairie chickens are tough and that it takes a full, heavy charge to drop them.

I've seen chickens knocked sideways and keep flying. Also, you never know the exact line the birds will take from roost to field. They may be off 30 yards from the line they held yesterday, so you must have enough gun and heavy enough charge to make up for this distance. This means, then, that chickens can be long-range targets.

They aren't the only birds in those prairie hills, either. A friend of mine said he wanted to hunt Kansas and asked if I knew anyone who could direct him about. I sided him up with Culbertson.

The next morning they entered a prairie chicken field and the hunter asked Jim, "What would be here in all this desolation?"

Jim answered, "Everything."

"Everything?" the guy countered.

"Yeah," said Jim, "Here you'll get bobwhites, pheasants, prairie chickens, and in season, doves."

The hunter scoffed but followed Jim. By noon he had all three legal birds in his bag (doves were out of season).

Have fun with chickens. They'll keep you coming back for more.

Hungarian Partridge and Sharp-Tail Grouse

T HESE ARE TWO REMARKABLE BIRDS that provide great dog training in summer and excellent hunting come fall and winter. They're found on the Dakota prairies, on into central Canada, and even up to Alaska. Paul Johnsgard, the eminent ornithologist, talks of a *plains* or *prairie* sharp-tail and differentiates its regions. That's vital for him, but cutting it too slim for our purposes. Yet, his *plains* and *prairie* bird is the one we most generally encounter when hunting from northern New Mexico, up through the Dakotas, and on into Alberta.

I've been privileged to know Dr. Johnsgard. I even charred a perfectly good steak on the backyard barbecue on my old Kansas farm, yet went ahead and served it to him anyway. I recall his enthusiasm in discussing grouse and quail waned after dinner, but he was so far out of my league that I probably missed the nuances that indicated I was a poor host and he could have used a Pepcid.

SUMMERING ON THE PRAIRIE

For the past 100 years, most big-time bird-dog trainers following the field-trial circuit—mostly from Dixie—have summered on these prairies, getting their charges into continued contact with these two launch-and-sputter-and-land-and-fly-again birds.

I'll explain. It's the nature of young birds from each year's hatch to hide in dense cover, essentially wait too long before a dog's inquiry, then launch, only to fly a short distance and land. The dogs are told to relocate by the handler, and the birds are bumped again. This gives a novice pup repeated opportunities not only to honor wing and shot but to pay keen attention to the birds' departure so he can take the gunner to the birds' new hideout. This bump and run is repeated over and over until the thoughtful trainer calls off the quest.

Remember, it's hot there in the summer, and all the participants in this ritual—horses, trainers, helpers, dogs, and birds—all tire and dehydrate. Add that to the fact that the spear grass is hearty and high at this time of year—just level with the dog's mouth and nose—and the pros must maintain constant vigilance.

SPEAR GRASS

Know what spear grass does. It's a grass that produces awns built upon a small, sharp spear. That spear can penetrate a dog anywhere, but most vitally in the respiratory channel. Beneath the point of the spear, stiff fibers (spears) catch tissue and migrate through the body as muscle or tissue is contracted and expanded.

The late M. Wayne Willis, my long-ago hunting buddy and world-class outdoor artist, had one of his Llewellyn setters get spear grass in a front leg. It migrated through the dog's body—you can sometimes follow the abscesses or possibly track them by x-ray—and exited at the hip. All this happened while a veterinarian was chasing it with surgery to the near death of the dog and at a cost of thousands of dollars. The dog survived but was off its game ever more.

LOOKING CLOSE

Sharp-tails and Huns live in punishing cover, ground so rough an English springer spaniel (a dog of choice for many) must actually leap, dig in, and root out the quarry. Take silver buffalo berry as an example. It's tangled and thorny, and an English springer spaniel will emerge with cut lips, bleeding nose, and matted eyes.

But put a class bird dog on these birds and he'll point from afar, then let the gunner walk about and kick them up; or if the dog's point is loose and lacks power, the birds (especially the Huns) will run before they fly.

When either sharp-tails or Huns do make their move and loft, they give gunners an explosion and swiftness that even outmatches bobwhites. The birds hold a tight pattern, which can prompt a gunner to flock shoot and miss the whole shebang. Both birds will be found during hunting season in mixed prairie grass, row crops, and weed fields. The sharp-tail will generally enter heavier brush than Huns will.

HUNGARIAN PARTRIDGE

The Hun is the third bird successfully imported to this country, the other two being the chukar and pheasant. Despite its name, the bird did not actually come from Hungary but from Russia, Sweden, and Germany. Hungary provided a scant part of the release.

Interestingly enough, the bird was introduced near the spot where the pheasant was let go: Oregon.

Hun cocks weigh about 13 ounces, measure about 13 inches, and

are identified on the wing by their rust-colored outer tail feathers, the inner tail feathers being gray.

In hand, the bird shows a brown cap and ear patch with a cinnamon face. The breast and upper belly are gray highlighted with chestnut crescents. The bird's back is gray to brown, with darker wings that reveal white streaks. As always, the female is similar but more drab.

These birds are generally located in great grasslands and semi-desert venues. They prefer bunchgrass and sagebrush areas near cultivated crops. They avoid woodlands, but take to brushy areas. During winter the birds form a roosting circle—heads to the outer perimeter—just as do bobwhites. This gives them 360 degrees of vigilance, plus group body heat to keep flock members warm. If conditions get really rough, or the snow is deep and the temperature plummeting, they can burrow under snow and stay snug.

When first detected by predators, the genetic disposition of these birds is to scat, to run in an erratic course that defies good aim with a gun. The eventual covey bust is more dramatic than even that of the bobwhite. And once aloft, the birds may cover a half mile before setting—only to take off running, again.

Any attempt to follow the birds and poke around their relocation is futile. By the time the hunter covers anywhere from an eighth to a quarter mile, the birds are long gone.

Another tactic of the elusive Hun is to beat toward a prominent hill and land on the far slope. That way the hunter has no idea which way the flight turned upon landing or whether the birds ran in a straight line. Another maneuver they use to outwit the hunter is to stick close, let the hunter pass, then backtrack.

During times of rest, the bird prefers knolls where it can survey the landscape. Yet they can surprise you and hide in row crops where you've entered to jump sharp-tails. If found in grain, the birds will do the same as pheasants: run to an edge and loft. No bird likes to exit to a bare stretch of dirt, cement, or asphalt.

SHARP-TAIL GROUSE

These birds are a whole different deal. Sure, you'll find them almost anywhere you find Huns, but sharp-tails give you an entirely different

escape. Once they're airborne, they set a straight course, alternately beating their wings, then setting them to soar, until they glide to their next haunt.

Sharp-tails can be found all the way from Canada to southern Colorado and laterally from Michigan to Oregon.

The adult male measures some 18 inches, has a wing span of 20 inches, and weighs about 2 pounds. The bird strongly resembles its southern cousin, the greater prairie chicken. By holding strange-looking birds in hand and trying to figure out what they were, I've even come to believe that the two birds occasionally cross breed.

The pure-bred bird has a black line from the bill through the eye. Both hen and cock bear striking resemblance: their cheeks and throat being white, bellies and sides white with black darts, and backs mottled black. Their wings are dark brown with a white pattern. Both birds sport a yellow comb above the eye, and on each side of the male's neck is an invisible air sac that can be seen only when inflated, at which time it appears pale purple. Both sexes are feathered to the base of their toes, and the white underparts are the outstanding characteristic noted in flight. These birds got their name due to their narrow, pointed tails, which are white edged.

Now you may think you've seen some heavy-duty dancing, but until you come upon a dancing sharp-tail, you ain't seen nothing yet. This guy gets with it.

You'd think he'd gone nuts with all his frenzy. But what he's doing is making it mighty plain he'll fight any male competitors anyplace, anytime, anywhere. All the antics are intended to attract a mate. So the male jumps, cackles, rattles his erected tail, calls out a great repertoire of sounds, and inflates his eye combs and neck sac.

When picking out a housing tract, sharp-tails prefer brushy and woody cover with mixed stands of hardwoods and conifers. If the copse contains aspen, they'll pay double rent. Aspens are their favorite trees. Another area they look for is clumped stands of woods and relatively sparse, far-flung forests.

Sharp-tails do not roost in trees overnight during winter. Instead, they scoop out snow burrows and, lacking snow, do the same thing in soft or moist earth.

These birds will eat grain as long as it lasts, but when the snow is deep they'll turn to buds of trees, twigs, and various tree fruits. They'll fly past miles of nature's abundance to dine on catkins and buds of birch and aspen.

DIFFERENCE IN SEASON

Especially during hunting season, and at other times, these birds prefer to congregate on knolls and keep an eye on the surrounding countryside. But as noted, once you roust sharp-tails from their lookouts they will give you a direct flight to their predesignated bail-out.

During summer the bird-dog trainers praise these birds for helping to get their dogs ready for the fall field-trial circuit back in the states.

WOLF WILLOWS

Big-time pointers and setters run a continuous race, what I call a stretched-out quest. So here's this broad, flat ground for them to have a go at it. Interspersed here and there on these flats are depressions blown out by constant prairie winds, or dusted out by itching buffalo years past.

The rains came and filled in these depressions, thus supporting the growth of what the Canadians call *wolf willows*. This, of course, is a misnomer: The trees are aspens and several varieties of poplar.

Dogs learn to run to these wolf willows because the sharp-tails hole up there: escaping from the prairie heat, secure in their humid environment, hidden from view by the stands of trees.

TRAINING

When the young birds are eventually flushed from these clumps of timber, they make an erratic, twittering flight, eager to set down in any stand of grass or copse of brush at the first opportunity.

Most important, the covey does not stay together. Instead, the birds scatter in flight and, upon landing, provide the dog and trainer invaluable opportunities to locate and handle singles.

What it all means is this: The dogs get constant bird work from young sharp-tail grouse. This is a rare event, especially since the trainers are putting their dogs on wild birds.

HUNTING

Let's say you come back in the fall to hunt these birds. If it's a hot opening day, the birds will stick to those buffalo willows. Then it's a matter of hunting those willows and following up on singles that fly to the nearest cover.

But let opening day be cool, and, Ha! The grouse leave the bluffs and keep a mighty distance between them and anything that moves. Now the birds are scattered on the prairie, not holed up in a stand of woods, and they are mighty elusive. Slam a car door and see what happens.

By the following weekend, after the opening-day hunters have had their fill, the birds can be found in hedgerows, along edges of cultivated crops and, yes, once more on their hilltops, surveying their surroundings.

DETAIL

To maximize your success when conditions get this way, you'll need a long-range, heavy-hitting gun, with high-impact shells—No. 4s, 5s and 6s.

You'll also need marathon legs, good lungs, and lots of water for you and your dog. Call the dog in often, give him drinks, and he'll run all day. But let the dog heat up and you'll find there's not enough water in the Missouri River to cool him down.

Sharp-tail and Hun grounds often contain pheasants, so you have a chance for a three-way bag.

Remember the spear grass: If it's a factor at this late date (during hunting season), the dog can possibly work during the early morning hours. Later than that the spears harden and become a menace.

Blue Grouse

THE BLUE GROUSE is my bird. I love this bird, love him as much for what he is as for what he does, and where he does it. One summer, while hunting at 10,000 feet, Mike Gould and Gary Ruppel, his sidekick and a puppy specialist from Kiowa, Colorado, introduced me to this bird. Mike's an innovator, a custom gun-dog trainer, who had a miracle Lab named Web. You know, this dog could practically survey the land, identify all of nature's flora and fauna, read minds, and hold psychiatry sessions with you lying on the forest floor, absorbing that high, bright Colorado sun.

In those days, Gould's kennels were in Carbondale, Colorado,

although he's since relocated to the Nez Perce country of Kamiah, Idaho.

Mike had a string of classy Elhew English pointer pups, and he wanted them in constant contact with wild birds. So he camped on the flat tops, 10,000 feet up in the Rockies, and daily cast Web to find a covey of blues. That'd only take a minute; then Web would stand there, looking at the birds, waiting for Mike's pups to show up.

Just a minute: Because Web was able to stand there like that, some people might say that this bird is like a fool's hen. But think a minute. In such total isolation, why should the birds fear encroachment? Let one shot be heard and you'll not find this covey until next spring. That's how foolish a blue grouse really is.

When Mike arrived with his pointers and Gary brought in his various pups in training and all dogs were on point, Web would retire, and Mike would steady Web's pack, do whatever was necessary—like picking one dog up and bringing him in closer—and then walk about and loft the birds.

Mike and Gary would keep the pups steady and give them multiple opportunities to watch the covey remnant and singles down. No shots were ever fired.

It wasn't necessary to rework a covey or even locate the singles, since Web would already have another covey located. Mike called Web a *strike* dog. And Web is the only Lab I've ever met so named, and so employed. He was one in a million. God rest his glorious soul.

LET'S LOOK AT THIS BIRD

The blue grouse is the largest of its species in the western states and provinces. He ranges from Alaska, down through western Canada, into eastern Washington, Oregon, and California. He's also found in the mountain country of Montana, Idaho, Nevada, Arizona, and Wyoming.

Females measure about 18 inches long and males average 20 inches, though they can go to 22.5 inches. Males and females are alike in appearance, both having squared tails with grayish tips.

The males' backs are gray with pronounced vermiculation, highlighted with brown and black peppering. The flanks and undertail coverts show white markings, and feathering reaches down the legs to the toes. Males also have bare skin over the eyes, which are yellow

A blue grouse in hand.

to yellow orange. Males can also display a bare neck patch that varies from deep yellow to purple. Females also have these bare-skin spots, but their overall body color is more brown.

Now I'm talking here about brown this and brown that and brown everything. But to have the dog fetch to hand and stand there and admire the bird close, well, it's brown, like a hen pheasant or prairie chicken.

But wait a minute. A field-trial mug on my desk shows some 40 separate blue grouse tail feathers. Let's look at one: It may appear brown, or even black, but it's general hue is really cadet gray—gray with chevrons of repetitive, mottled brown and black with a 1-inch band of black at the tail's end and a final swipe of gray. So what's brown, especially when we call this a blue grouse? You go get one and tell me.

But mind you, there are eight subspecies of blue grouse, and the one I'm in constant contact with is the dusky blue, maybe that's why I see cadet gray.

HABITAT

The favorite resting site of these birds is male aspen stands. In late June or July you can determine the sex of an aspen tree by looking at the buds. The buds of the male are larger than those of the female and much richer in protein, fat, and minerals. Blue grouse seem to avoid the female trees when it comes to dining.

If you want to increase your chances of sighting blue grouse, follow the range of the true fir and the Douglas fir. As a matter of fact, the blue grouse range is coincidental with that of the Douglas fir. Blues range from 7,000 to 10,000 feet in fall and winter. Fall? I've found them at 10,000 feet in August.

MIGRATION

The deal is, blues migrate. They winter at the highest elevation that stands timber. This is high and cold country, where their principal

A hunter and pointer take time out from a blue grouse hunt. The 10,000-foot elevation can affect dogs as well as people.

diet is needles. They concentrate on true and Douglas fir, consuming seeds, buds, needles, and twigs. I don't know much, but I've heard of only one other creature filling up on needles in the winter and that's the black bear just before it hibernates. But then, I'm a hunter and not a naturalist or zoologist.

When spring arrives, the mating urge drives the blues down the slope. There are reports that they travel up to 30 miles, and their descent won't stop until they find relatively open and dry cover, characterized by shrubs with lots of bare ground. That reminds me of bobwhites. The migration, on the other hand, makes you think of the mountain quail. Remember?

Blue grouse choose both elevation and cover that will provide their young with insects during the first 10 days of their lives. An optimal diet includes ants and beetles. As the young mature they switch to berries. Come August, they all head back up the mountain.

COURTSHIP

Before the chicks are born, the cocks must woo the hens—which, for blue grouse, is an elaborate ritual called hooting. The males hoot from ground clearings or high tree branches, boasting *this is my turf; stay out.* As the cock's behavior is designed to drive away males, it must also attract a mate. This calls for a great production of movements, calls, and body posture.

Possibly the most complicated and dramatic of all bird courtships, it can be likened to a counterculture orgy. It doesn't occur during hunting season, though, so we'll forgo the details; but I tell you, it's something.

HOW TO HUNT

There are several ways to hunt blue grouse: Put bird dogs on him and shoot over points; send flushing Labs or springers in and roust him out of his hideaway; or just take off, cross-country, hoping for voluntary flushes. I've done all three. Because of the elevation and the inclines, it's tough hunting for an older hunter, but the young can take it in stride. Besides, there are plenty of fallen logs to sit on so you can regain your composure.

Blue grouse will also run to a cliff and launch downward to the valley floor. They loft high, which causes many to shoot where they think the bird is going. Since the bird usually dives suddenly, it's generally best to shoot under.

I've found blue grouse with sage hens, so you can have a mixed bag. As a matter of fact, the sage hen's territory generally coincides with that of the blue grouse.

Since you can get a point on these birds, No. 7½ shot serves the purpose. If the birds are spooky and rising early, switch to No. 6s or 4s. A lightweight 20 gauge is the gun of choice because of its reduced weight. Carry it either in automatic or two tubes.

Keep water with you, though you'll come upon freshets and rivulets. And even in that high wilderness, you can suddenly encounter a constantly running, store-bought water pipe—erected by whom?

THE BEAUTY OF IT ALL

Nowhere will you have a more beautiful hunt. In early morning you can watch the sunrise touch each successive peak, then slide down to the valley depths. There's always a wafting breeze cresting the cliffs, and you'll see the harrier hawk smoothly handle the currents above you. The distant vistas are captivating.

The whole panorama can be so beautiful that you'll be hard put to weigh it all out. Are you having the best of all hunts? Or are you experiencing a magnificence in nature that no other place could match?

13

Sage Grouse

T HE SAGE GROUSE is one big bird that doesn't live on Sesame Street. Startling to confront the first time, the sage grouse seems like a desert turkey without glitz: just a big, old plain bird, dust colored and gangly. Cockbirds can weigh 8 pounds and be 30 inches in length, roughly the size of a specklebelly goose.

I find this bird a dud to hunt and a flop in the pot. Why? I'm not that fond of sage, and this bird practically lives on it. Since I won't shoot anything I don't eat, I leave this bird alone.

The last time I shot a sage grouse and tried to cook it, I left it on the stove for seven days. Each time I poked it with a fork it proved

tougher than a cavalry saddle. I gave up. Who's to say you won't have better luck or that you're a better cook?

The sage grouse struts and displays to intimidate competitive suitors and to attract hens (yes, they are polygamous). This ritual is performed on large strutting grounds (called leks), where the cock inflates himself to exaggerated proportions with the highlight being the white, puffed-up oval of feathers that runs from his upper back down both sides of his neck and then falls in pendulums several inches before his chest. All this is showcased with an absolute, upright position and a spread, spiked tail. The olive green sacs on the back and breast are expanded and collapsed, with a resulting popping sound.

Distinguishing characteristics aflight are a black belly patch and long, sprig tail. The overall color is a dark gray-brown.

Where They Live

The birds range from Canada through Washington, Oregon, and California—nowhere approaching the Pacific—and inland through Idaho, Utah, Colorado, Nevada, New Mexico, Wyoming, and Montana. There's also a smattering of birds in the Dakotas and a wee bit in Nebraska.

The birds will be anywhere there is sage grass. This grass must stand above the snow line for both cover and feed in the winter. Cocks are the first to leave these wintering grounds and head for their leks. The distance between their winter homes and strutting grounds can be 100 miles, which might qualify grouse as migratory.

Following the hatch, peeps favor ants, weevils, beetles, and grasshoppers, on essentially moist grounds. During summer, all grouse feed heavily on dandelions.

How to Hunt

When hunting season opens, sage grouse will be found anywhere you find chukars and blue grouse. A dog is imperative for the hunt, since grouse are seldom brought to hand without a point. You might kick up a surprised grouse, but the rule is, no point, no game.

Dogs don't take to sage grouse all that fast. At lower elevations there are intense heat and miles of barren flats to contend with. Plus, when the dog enters the bird's scent cone, he's encountering a very strange odor.

Any bird dog will do. Cast your favorite. Even Labs can flush the sage grouse under certain conditions. The most success will come over a long-winded, ground-covering, full-bored nose pointer or setter. Don't forget the Brittany and all the European versatile pointers, however.

When a sage grouse lofts, it's like a B-52 getting airborne, or so it seems. The bird is actually flying faster than a bobwhite and picks up speed as he beats and then glides down a slope. It takes a big-time impact to bring one of these birds down, and you'd better look sharp, for these birds blend in perfectly with the ground cover.

Dog and hunter can walk for only so long. But take heart, for now you can scout a waterhole and make a hide. If birds are using the place, you'll find tracks. The usual routine sees sage grouse visit water several times a day. If nooning, the birds loaf just outside the water tank area.

I use the term *water tank,* but running water is also found in irrigation troughs, tailing ponds, creeks, seeps, and so on.

There'll be broad expanses where you'll not find a drop of water. So you'll need to tote what you drink, plus a supply for Pup.

Since you're shooting over points, you can reduce your burden. Select a 20 gauge with low-brass No. 4s and 6s. Should you drop one, don't you think Pup should mutiny if you insist that the dog fetch such a huge bird all the way back to the truck?

Keep in mind that you can get lost in these great featureless flats. Ever think of carrying a helium-filled balloon you can hoist over your pickup? I have, and it works.

Carrying a compass and a Global Positioning System (GPS) isn't such a bad idea, either. Just make sure you know how to use them.

14

Woodcock

YOU'VE SEEN HIM in a thousand brandy commercials—the gray sideburns and crushed hat, the squared mustache constantly evened with the back of an index finger. He's wearing a great waxed coat with wide elastic sewn into the handkerchief pocket so two follow-up shells can be brought quick to hand. Then there are the flared breeches, the cavalry boots, and the Llewellyn setter, wet to the skin, shivering by his left leg.

It can mean but one thing: Gentry drink brandy and hunt woodcock.

A WORM, ANYONE?

Surprisingly, we had woodcock in Kansas, and nonelite as I was, I'd get one now and then when going for quail. Lord knows, I never set

out to hunt a bird that spent its life with its nose stuck in mud siphoning for earthworms.

I remember Darrell Kincaid, an oil man, retriever enthusiast, and pump-gun expert, created a club where if you could double on woodcock in his presence, Darrell would put you on an honor roll and give you a silver hat pin. I never did do well in front of Darrell. For certain, I never got the woodcock pin; once I even fell backward out of Darrell's duck boat.

DOG TRAINING

I love any wild bird that's a benefit to gun-dog training. Woodcock migrate twice a year: north to south and south to north. When the birds come north in early spring, a dog handler can get in some exceptional bird work. The birds stick, the dogs learn to honor their scent cone—even if they don't like the smell—and they learn, as well, the necessity of being steady to wing and (blank) shot.

IN APPEARANCE

The woodcock is a dirt-colored bird with eyes set high and far back in the head so it can see 360 degrees while eating. The bird has a big head to accommodate those wide-spaced eyes and to support that railroad-spike proboscis.

The woodcock, which you'll learn is called a Timberdoodler—for his phenomenal flight—weighs just over 6 ounces and measures 11 inches in length. It flies only 13 miles an hour, but that doesn't mean a thing. This is a master aerialist that occupies only that piece of air that your shot never encounters. I mean this guy can put a grapevine between you and he in one billionth of a second. There was a time I called the woodcock the bark bird, for I had so much of the stuff flying around.

HABITAT

The fact that the woodcock lives in swamps, mud bogs, marsh skirtings, wide creek meanderings, and other generally bottomless places means the vegetation abounds. It is this vegetation that conceals his flight, no matter where he's going or how fast you're shooting. I don't know if anyone ever got a video camera on a woodcock upside down, but I swear he's capable of any type of flight—even penetrating and exiting tree trunks.

APPEARANCE

Now get this: We're talking about a shorebird here, but hunting him as upland game. He comes to hand Van Dyke brown, with but a hint of a tail and rounded wings. The bird is nocturnal but is available for daylight hunts. He explodes on the rise with whistling wings and disappears before you can get your gun shouldered.

DOG WORK

Any dog that hunts close will do well on woodcock. A woodcock will let a dog stand beside him all day, but once a hunter appears, it's adios. Since the bird sleeps during the day, its bed is understandably deeply concealed and has endured the test of time. A dog must hunt close to puzzle out the bird's bedroom.

Though must gun dogs will point a woodcock, few will fetch it to hand. It stinks. Look closely when a woodcock falls to your gun, as you may have to retrieve it yourself.

GUNNING

The bird favors heavy timber and masses of limbs, and he has the ability to fly where any other bird would kill himself. You must seek him out with a lightweight gun: a 20 or 28 gauge shooting No. 7½s. If limbs soak up the light shot, then go heavier because you might be able to knock some of the stuff down and still have enough firepower to get the bird.

Be careful of your footing—this is slide-and-fall country. Sometimes dogs get into boggy mud that cakes to their feet, so that they spend undue time scraping at the stuff, even chewing at it with their teeth.

RANGE

Woodcock can be found from the Great Lakes down through Louisiana and on eastward to Georgia, then up through New England. The woodcock is not a resident of Florida.

The woodcock's courting flight is unique and spectacular. In early morning and at late dusk, you'll come upon the cock in an open grassy spot, where he alternates his display of strutting with a sky-ward zoom that culminates in a spiral back to earth. The mute twit-tering sound that you often hear during this spiral is apparently made by the wings.

No other bird may prove as testing for you as a woodcock. These birds are hard to find, hard to manage, hard to hunt, and hard to bring to hand. But they're also hard to overlook.

15

Ruffed Grouse

WHILE IN THE COMPANY of ruffed grouse hunters, I've often felt a silent consensus: *If we weren't hunting ruffed grouse we wouldn't be hunting at all.*

The ruffed grouse has taken on many dimensions, even to becoming a national mascot: The bird was involved in many incidents that became the basis of our national pride.

He was there to greet the Pilgrims. He was in the outskirts of Philadelphia at the signing of the Declaration of Independence. And he could be heard across the sweep of the White House lawn, drumming in the brush of the Potomac, when Lincoln signed the Emancipation Proclamation.

The Northeast doesn't circumscribe the bird's total range, either.

The ruffed grouse is found from Alaska, through all the Canadian provinces, completely across the upper states of America, and as far south as Tennessee and the Carolinas. So he was there at the firing on Fort Sumter as well as at the surrender at Appomattox.

RULES OF TRADITION

There are many upper-crust "requirements" accompanying a ruffed grouse hunt. The dog better be a white- and black-ticked Llewellyn setter. The gun should be a side-by-side, dainty and lightweight as a fawn's leg. At no time would a gentleman shoot anything more lethal than No. 7½ shot.

Despite these "rules," I love ruffed grouse, and I love to hunt ruffed grouse. And I bring them to hand with Labs, curs, and all sorts of beloved canines, shooting heavy guns with industrial-strength shells. You see, I'm not upper crust, so anything goes!

OTHER DIMENSIONS

But there is this: Since all my life I've hunted the barrens of the West, you put me in those eastern timber tangles and I'll hope for a chainsaw to clear a path. I just don't like the idea of missing anything I've worked so hard to get, as a ruffed grouse.

Okay, maybe my reference to a chainsaw is a little crude, so let me put it all into perspective. To hunt is a privilege. I don't mean some right given by the state, but given by God for his placing the game here and giving us Genesis as our guideline.

Furthermore, hunters have many obligations to the game they pursue. Foremost, they must study it, learn everything about it: where it lives, what it eats, how it hides, its physical needs for each time of the day and for the season.

Only when hunters know the game so well they can predict what it's going to do and dupe it into their gun range do they have the right to go for it.

What a hunter hunts is based only on the individual's ability to go afield, knowing how to survive there, how to use the equipment of the hunt, and honor the game sought more than anything else. Ultimately it is the hunter's obligation to sustain the game during times of peril.

THE BIRD

No bird is honored more than the ruffed grouse.

The male grouse can weigh in at approximately 1¼ pounds and measure 19 inches in length. It is gorgeous in display, with a pronounced fanned tail of many concentric rings and a great brown stripe near the terminus of the fan. About the cock's neck is a huge ruff, and his wings protrude and droop to the ground.

Scrutinize him in flight and you'll see brown spots at the bottom, back of the neck and a patch of brown and white at the inside, bottom of the wings. The legs have no feathers.

Remember, the ruffed grouse has two distinct color phases: inclined toward red in the South and toward gray in the North.

Once again we have the grand display of the grouse courtship. Here the ruffed grouse seeks a hollow log, or several of them, mounts one, then "drums" by beating the air rapidly with his wings. The ruffed grouse also struts, especially to rush at an encroaching male.

The bird subsists on fruits, leaves, and buds, with the young preferring insects. Grouse live in open woods and parks during spring and summer, and conifers in winter. Stands of balsam, poplar, and paper birch overlie its habitat. As with other woods birds, you can't go wrong checking stands of aspen in search of ruffed grouse.

Wintertime sees the birds roosting in evergreen trees or burrowing under snow. They require standing water.

HONORING THE SCENT CONE

Delmar Smith, the man who made the Brittany a field-trial dog in America, was campaigning in New England, having entered a horseback trial for ruffed grouse.

His Brittany had been trained to stop at the absolute, outermost hint of a scent cone. The dog did. Delmar dismounted and walked the bird up, firing his blank pistol.

One of the two judges coaxed his horse forward and told Delmar, "In a lifetime of hunting ruffed grouse, that's the most perfect job I've ever seen for a man on horseback handling a grouse."

That night, traveling down the road, Delmar confided in me, "That man shouldn't have been surprised. All you have to do to get good points on ruffed grouse is make sure the dog doesn't crowd the bird's space."

That's the ultimate rule when hunting ruffed grouse. Don't let the bird feel as if you're pushing him. He can't stand it, won't stand it, and will loft away quickly in a whir of wings.

FEEDING

Don't forget to drop in on the bird's favored restaurants during hunting season. Have your dog check all stands of aspens, willows, catkins, hazelnut, wild cherry, and apple. There the birds eat buds, fruit, leaves, and twigs.

Remember to cast Pup about and have him investigate snow banks closely. Who knows if the birds have burrowed in to keep warm. If they have, stand back because you're going to get a mighty launch.

COLOR AND BELLS

Since grouse frequent heavy cover, it behooves both hunter and dog to outfit themselves with bells. Of course, if you've got a rock-bottom steady bird dog that will not move on point, then what are you going to hear? So the hunter must walk about, following the tinkling bells, but finally, if the bells disappear, the hunter must shout out. The one thing you don't want is a lost dog.

Dress yourself and Pup with lots of fluorescent orange clothing. We want both of you to see each other as much as possible, and we surely want both of you to be conspicuous to any other hunter.

RAINY WEATHER

Ruffed grouse live in perennially bad weather. Seven-day rains are common. And rain hunting is a lost cause. Bad weather is especially hard on ruffed grouse because it destroys the apples. If fall is late, however, the apples will still be clinging to the trees, and the grouse will have no way of harvesting them. They avoid open orchards at such times.

A ruffed grouse hunter refreshes his setters at a stream before going back into the heavy cover.

You should also know that ruffed grouse don't want to eat hard apples: They prefer them mushy and fermented, which is another reason they wait for the apples to fall.

The alternative is for the hunter to concentrate on intertangled and impenetrable cover. That's a downer, day after day, with everything dripping wet.

So pray for apples on the ground, or dry weather.

In any case, know there are some hunters who demand you look good doing it.

CHAPTER

Mourning Dove

THE FIRST TIME I went afield with my old friend, wildlife painter Wayne Willis, it was for mourning doves. Since Wayne was in charge, he loaded me up, then drove a few miles south of town, staying on the main highway. Soon he stopped, exited the car, and started walking into a weed field with dilapidated road signs and soybeans planted on the far side.

Wayne carried a Browning 20 gauge in his right hand and a galvanized bucket in the other.

I assumed his plan was to enter the bean field, sit on the bucket, and shoot doves. But there were so many doves trading back and forth enroute that Wayne had his legal limit in the bucket before he ever left the weeds.

How could I forget it? He'd throw up the Browning, steady the forepiece with the hand holding the bucket, sweep, shoot, then scoop up the fall. We had no dog to do the fetching.

I knew the national average for doves was four shots per bird. Wayne was the one person who didn't know it, shooting one shot for one bird eight straight times.

THE ABUNDANT BIRD WITH THE MAXIMUM HARVEST

The mourning dove is the most abundant bird, with the maximum harvest, in the United States: Some 20,000,000 a year are brought to hand. If the national average is actually four shells per bird, that's 80 million shells.

These birds may be found from Canada into Mexico. I've had them on my property everywhere I ever lived, and right now they are roosting in my chimney in the blast furnace of south Nevada.

THE NEST

Doves build nests that couldn't pass the least stringent housing inspector's test. Their nests show all the planning of a floodjam, with sticks jutting every which way, shattered leaves, feathers of any kind—just airy, flimsy, chaotic, slapstick, negligence.

Unless this nest blows down, I'll show you what's expected of it. Mature doves can lay two eggs in this nest three to four times a year. The young grow up fast, so the egg laying just keeps going on.

The kicker is that this year's young may also mate and lay two eggs, meaning some 10 doves could have been hatched to one set of parents, and at least one of their young having mated with a dove from another family.

We may worry from time to time about loss of some particular species in the wild, but I don't think we'll ever include mourning doves.

RANGE

I've encountered doves from sea level to 8,000 feet. I've found them in deep coniferous forests, deserts, hedgerows, grain fields, truck farms, orchards, deciduous timber stands, and any place people frequent.

Spring sees the birds nesting in lower elevations, and depending on wealth of feed and water, the birds may be laying their last eggs in September.

CALLED ON ACCOUNT OF RAIN

If there is one truth about doves, it's this. I've never completed a dove season. Why? Because a rain inevitably pushes the birds away. I mean it. No matter where I've been, it's the same old story. Dove season is great, every day gets greater, then one night a cool rain will sweep through the country and before you can get to the field that morning, the birds are gone.

They are the most fair-weather birds in the world. Yet, and get this, I've lived in freezing country where late-born doves won't migrate. So some doves can take the cold and others bottom up at the first cool mist.

HOW TO HUNT

Doves will present an infinite variety of hunts to the individual who wants to experience all their craftiness. I like to take a stand by a pond or tank and shoot them as they come to water. Such pass shooting results from knowing about their daily activities. Once you learn their flight lanes, the key is to then make a hide and catch them going to grain fields or visiting gravel sources for their gizzards.

To make your hunt even easier—to maximize your success—choose a sesame seed or sunflower seed field. Now you just set up on their two favorite foods.

Kansas is a haven for doves. And here they come, being able to attain 60 miles an hour just for the fun of it, only now they've got that tail wind behind them, and move over jets! You think you have coordination, eyesight, muscle control, and balance. Hah. Get ready for some lessons in humiliation. You'll leave the field knowing you are the saddest shot who ever mounted a stock. Think seriously about seeing an eye doctor.

It's not because doves cruise at 60 miles an hour that you can't hit them. It's because they are aerial acrobats like none other. Study the doves and you'll see how testy a target a butterfly could be if it

A German short-haired pointer dives into the water after a dove that has dropped into the cattails.

flew 60 miles an hour. They sashay, dip, slide, climb, twist, reverse (I swear they do), and twirl. If there's anything a bird can't do on the wing, doves do it.

They also have an uncanny detection system, seeming to know exactly where you'll be found. At the slightest hint that they're right, they'll slam into a repertoire of maneuvers the Thunderbirds couldn't unravel.

Pass shooting is the most difficult, I assure you, and can be practiced only by the hunter who's spent all summer learning their flight lanes.

THE PARTY SHOOT

There is one type of hunt that has more popularity than any other, and that's party shooting grain fields in the South. You know, the good ol' boys: They've planned this hunt for months, invited every-body for miles about—even relatives from three states over.

A great groaning table may be hidden in the trees, festooned with sodas, lemonade, iced tea, corn on the cob, red beans and rice, fried chicken, berry pie, and more.

Around the field itself, all the shooters have taken a stand, hoping to get the best place depending on the direction of the wind. Every type of gun imaginable will be aimed skyward. All gauges, all makes, all chokes, and all shells. And there'll be a Lab tied to every ankle.

MIGRATORY DOVES

Doves are migratory game birds and under federal jurisdiction. Make sure you check out all the regulations before you hunt them. When the shooting is fast and furious, some people can be tempted to shoot more than they should. Don't do it!

Some hunters try to take their doves over a dog's point. That seldom happens. Doves flock in groups of two: love birds. In other words, they're not covey birds.

When a migration comes, they'll join up, but that's done quickly, and then the birds are gone.

Doves won't run before a dog, they'll flush, hearty and quickly. They'll startle you, so you just don't get all that much sport with a bird dog.

THE BIRD IN HAND

I know you can get the bird in hand and laud its iridescent col-oration; make great distinction. But I see the bird in flight: a gray bird with a heavy breast, small head, and pointed tail. It walks with a bobbing head, like a pigeon.

BUSH WHACKING

For bush whacking doves, choose a 20- or 28-gauge shotgun. The winds will demand the size of shot and charge of powder.

There isn't a farm boy who hasn't knocked a dove off a telephone line. But it is illegal to shoot in a public right-of-way. Remember that.

Remember This, Too

When pond or grain field hunting, the hunter needs a retriever to fetch from water or to search vast areas for a downed bird. This can be accomplished if the dog handler follows a few simple rules.

The dog must be kept cool at all times. Dove hunting is a hot-weather activity, though, so here's what we do. Leaving home, the dog should be transported in a cross-ventilated or air-conditioned vehicle. If this isn't possible, the dog should be stored in a crate with at least a 25-pound block of ice. He'll love it.

The Ice Block

When you get to your field or pond, walk, *I mean walk,* to your set-up, which is usually under a tree. Carry the ice block with you. Place it on the ground and let it start to melt. Now scoot the ice over and tell Pup to lie down in the puddle.

Before you do anything else, give Pup a drink. Then, 15 minutes later, refresh him again. Do the same thing in another 15 minutes. The point is, if you can keep Pup cool, he'll fetch for you all day. But if Pup ever gets hot, there's not enough water in Lake Mead to cool him down. If you reach that point, Pup will quit fetching.

Here's how it works. Pup's got a hot mouth to begin with. When his temperature goes up, his mouth gets hotter. Once the saliva gets hot, it turns to a gunk with the ability to pick up almost anything: grass, pebbles, grit, feathers, seeds, and so forth.

Keep a Water-Slick Mouth

Particularly annoying to Pup are dove feathers. They're flimsy, fuzzy, and easily soaked on their fringes. Now Pup rubs the side of his face in the grass. Grass! Now he's got more grass, plus feathers.

So the cycle goes. But if enough water is on hand, you can break the cycle. Pup once again attains a water-slick mouth. And when that happens, he'll be all too happy to fetch for you.

PUP AFIELD

If a puppy is in the field, hide the doves that are already in your possession. Store them in a water cooler, a gunny sack, whatever. Just don't let the puppy get feathers stuck all about and be put off doves for life.

As a matter of fact, of all the bird hunts available, a dove hunt would be the last hunt I'd choose to introduce a puppy to the sound of the gun, the taste of feather, the heat of the day, and the predictably long and boring waits for anything to happen.

Puppies want action; they have an attention span of seconds or minutes. When starting one, keep everything fast-paced and happy.

When the Hunt Is Over

YOU HANG YOUR COAT in the mud room, toss your mud-caked boots to side—it's all over. Tomorrow you'll clean your gun and stow the shells in the basement, but for now you look out the window at the dark that brings it all to an end.

Then you hear Pup at the back screen door. Knowing you've seen him, he serpentines his body, then presses himself close to the screen. You stand watching and remembering.

There'd been no hunt without him. Even if you took him for mountain quail and couldn't get within 20 yards of them, he still made the hunt memorable. He made it joyful.

Now you open the door and he enters to rise and place his paws on your chest. You thump his flank and tell him, "You're a good boy . . . you know that? Yes . . . a good boy."

He drops now and looks across the floor to see if anything's in his food bowl. You put on false airs, acting disappointed, "So that's all I mean to you, huh? Just a handout. And what did you ever do for that? Huh? Did you ever once earn a meal?"

The dog knows your game—he knows everything about you. Then you feed him, stand and watch him, and smile. Then you remember, he'll have to go to the vet tomorrow.

By switching to the night shift, taking sick leave, plus your accumulated vacation, you were able to hunt 30 days of a 60-day season. If Pup covered 8 miles a day, every day, he traveled 240 miles.

I know you stopped Pup every once in a while and checked his eyes and pads. You learned to saturate a handkerchief and pour water into his eyeballs, letting the debris pour out next to the nose. And upon finding a cracked toenail, I know you clipped it off. For should

Pup try running with a hanging nail, he'd be so sore the next morning that he couldn't get out of his crate.

You checked him daily for fox tail or spear grass, for awns stuck between his toenails and skin. You ran your finger all around and inside his lips, looking for anything that might have hung up there, or between the teeth.

If Pup's a male you should have daily checked the prepuce of his penis. It's amazing how debris can enter that cavity and cause inflammation, and how the same debris can rub the scrotum nearly bare. Females can also sore up quickly by dragging their teats and nipples through spiked row crops all the time.

What about the ears? Sure the stuff blows in there, the grasses and crop debris are flung in there, and you know to *never* stick anything in an ear to try and retrieve a foreign object. Never. That's a job for the vet. Same with the throat.

But what if you've never been that caring? that thoughtful? Well then you really know how much Pup needs veterinary attention!

You might even need a little doctoring yourself. I've had cactus stick me causing infection. I walked too long and too far in wet boots, and ended up with feet looking like prunes. What about frostbite? Or, just like Pup, the stuff that stuck deep inside the eyelids?

There are insect bites, allergies, plus toxic materials that you accidentally rubbed against. Doc will know.

Then there's the final need for another buddy that made every mile with you: your pickup. How many creek beds did you not just ford, but actually drive straight down? How many boulders did you slip off of? Yes, it was an ominous sound. And the mud! You can't even see the frame, it all looks like one great big glob.

Let's say that the hunt's not over until you, Pup, and your truck have all been checked out and cleared for another hunt come season.

Outdoor troubles mount. They build one upon the other. Get everything fixed for the next outing, since a hunt tests the best of everything.

Isn't that one of the reasons you're out there?

Index